COOK'S COLORING BOOK

COOK'S COLORING BOOK

Simple Recipes for Beginners

RACHEL LEWIS

GIBBS SMITH
TO ENRICH AND INSPIRE HUMANKIND

For my amazing family, friends, and everyone who encouraged me. You know who you are.

———————————————————

Manufactured in Hong Kong in January 2015 by Paramount Printing

First Edition
19 18 17 16 15   5 4 3 2 1

The cooking and baking activities suggested in this book may involve the use of sharp objects and hot surfaces. Parental guidance is recommended. The author and publisher disclaim all responsibility of injury resulting from the performance of any activities listed in this book. Readers assume all legal responsibility for their actions.

Published by
Gibbs Smith
P.O. Box 667
Layton, Utah 84041

1.800.835.4993 orders
www.gibbs-smith.com

Cover designed by Katie Jennings
Interiors designed by Rachel Lewis
Gibbs Smith books are printed on paper produced from sustainable PEFC-certified forest/controlled wood source. Learn more at www.pefc.org.

ISBN 13: 978-1-4236-3845-2

CONTENTS

INTRODUCTION

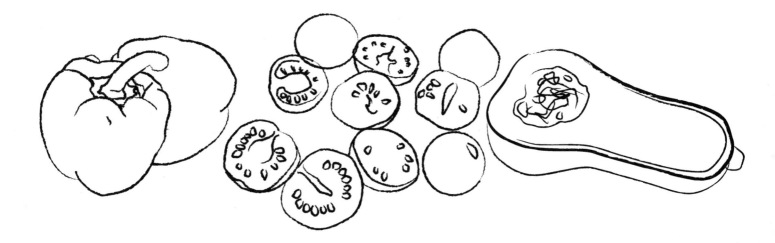

Some of my favorite things are cooking and drawing. These two don't often go together, but I do get very impatient while waiting for my food to be ready; I usually doodle all over the notes I've made on my recipe books and printouts. Cooking is my ultimate way of relaxing after a long, hard day—so is the unadulterated pleasure of picking up a pencil and just filling some lines with color. Most cookbooks always have such beautiful photography—this book isn't about that. This book isn't about sticking perfectly to a recipe—just how coloring books aren't about sticking between the lines. This book is about easy, go-to recipes that everyone can cook, especially young, beginning cooks, and make their own, no matter who you're feeding and when. It doesn't matter if it doesn't look how it's supposed to—food is for the pleasure of eating, and experimenting. Even if you don't stick between the lines.

BREAKFASTS

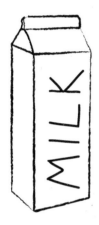

BREAKFAST BERRY SMOOTHIE

Using frozen berries keeps this smoothie thick and ice cold—the oatmeal adds substance and protein and keeps you going until lunch.

Serves 4

You will need:

1 small ripe banana

¾ cup (5 ounces) / 140 g frozen strawberries, blueberries, raspberries, or blackberries

½ cup (4 ounces) / 125 ml milk

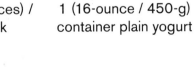

1 (16-ounce / 450-g) container plain yogurt

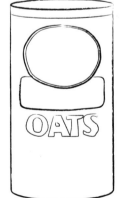

2 tablespoons (1 ounce) / 30 g uncooked oatmeal

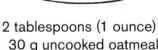

2 teaspoons honey, optional

WHAT TO DO:

1. Slice the banana into your food processor or blender and add berries of choice.

2. Pour in the milk and yogurt and blend until smooth.

3. Stir in the oatmeal and pour into 4 glasses.

4. Serve with a drizzle of honey on top.

Eggs Royale

A twist on the classic Eggs Benedict. Swapping the usual ham for smoked salmon makes this a truly luxurious weekend breakfast. If you don't want to make your own hollandaise sauce you can of course cheat and use store bought.

Serves 4

YOU WILL NEED:

3 tablespoons
(1 1/2 ounces) /
45 ml white wine
vinegar, divided

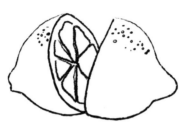

2 teaspoons lemon juice

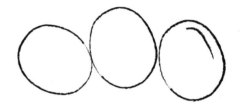

3 egg yolks

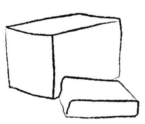

3/4 cup (5 ounces) /
140 g unsalted butter,
cut into small cubes

Salt and pepper, to taste

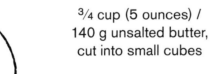

4 eggs

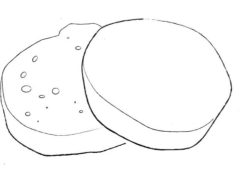

2 English muffins

8 slices smoked salmon

12

WHƏT TO DO:

1. Place a saucepan of water over high heat and bring to a simmer.

2. Add 1 tablespoon of vinegar into a bowl with the lemon juice and egg yolks and whisk by hand until light and frothy.

3. Place the bowl over the pan of hot water and keep whisking until it starts to thicken.

4. Gradually add in the butter, whisking constantly until thick, making sure the heat stays fairly low. If it looks like the sauce might separate, remove from heat and keep whisking. Season with a bit of salt and pepper and set aside.

5. Fill a shallow pan with about 2 inches / 5 cm of water, add the rest of the vinegar and a pinch of salt, and bring to a low simmer.

6. Crack each egg into a cup and swirl the water to create a small whirlpool; pour in each egg to the center in turn. The force of the water binds the egg together to create a neat poached egg. Cook each for about 3 minutes.

7. While the eggs are cooking, cut the muffins in half and toast them; placing 2 slices of salmon over each half.

8. Top each half with an egg and spoon the hollandaise over the top; sprinkle with pepper. Serve immediately.

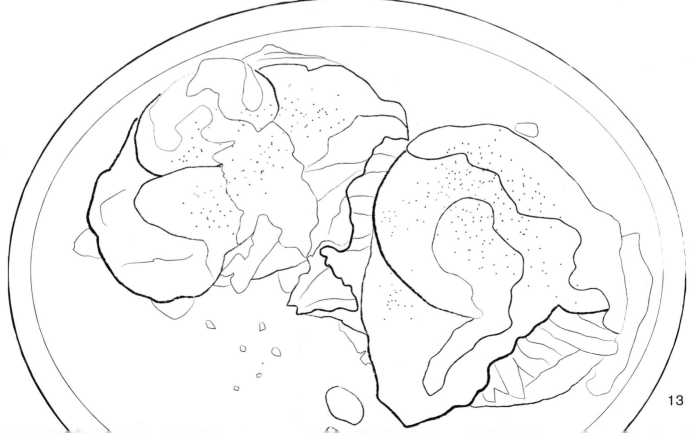

MEXICAN OMELETTE

Spice up your breakfast time with this Mexican spin on a classic egg dish—this should wake you up!

Serves 2

You will need:

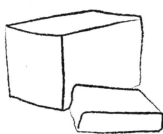

4 large eggs

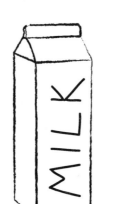

1/4 cup (2 ounces) / 60 ml milk

Salt and pepper, to taste

1 teaspoon dried oregano

2 tablespoons (1 ounce) / 30 g butter

1/2 cup (4 ounces) / 115 g chopped tomatoes

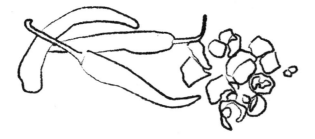

1/4 cup (2 ounces) / 60 g chopped green chiles, canned or fresh

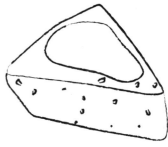

1/2 cup (2 ounces) / 60 g grated Pepper Jack cheese

What to do:

1. Whisk together the eggs, milk, and seasonings in a bowl.

2. Heat a small frying pan, add the butter, and melt over medium heat.

3. Spoon the egg mixture evenly over bottom of pan. As the omelette cooks, lift the edges with a spatula and mix the center so it's not too thick.

4. When the omelette is relatively solid, add the tomatoes, chiles, and cheese and continue cooking until the cheese melts.

5. Fold in half and serve!

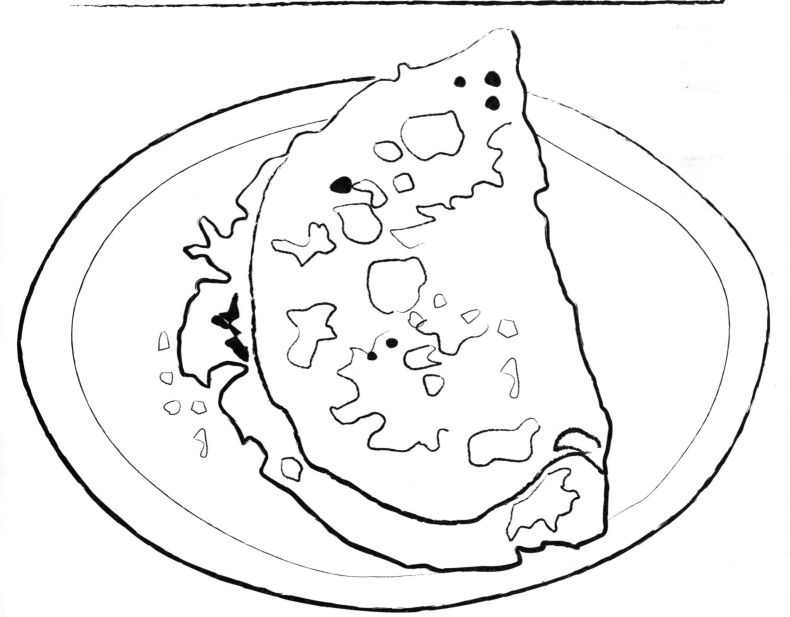

Tomato and Spinach Baked Eggs

A colorful brunch bursting with fresh ingredients and flavor—this is what Sundays were made for. The bacon and cheese is optional if you'd like to keep it healthy!

Serves 4

You will need:

1 tablespoon
canola oil

4 slices bacon, chopped

4 mini sweet
peppers, chopped

1 cup (8 ounces) / 225 g
mushrooms, chopped

Salt and pepper,
to taste

½ cup (4 ounces) /
115 g fresh spinach

1 (14-ounce / 400-g)
can chopped tomatoes

1 teaspoon dried chile flakes
1 teaspoon dried mixed
herbs of choice

1 tablespoon
plain yogurt

4 eggs

½ cup (2 ounces) / 60 g
grated cheddar cheese

WHaT To Do:

1. Preheat oven to 350 degrees F / 180 degrees C / gas mark 4.

2. Heat the oil in a frying pan and add the bacon, frying for 5 minutes.

3. Add the sweet peppers and mushrooms and fry until they start to brown.

4. Place the spinach in a colander, boil some water, and pour over the spinach to wash and wilt it.

5. Drain the chopped tomatoes through a sieve to get rid of any excess juice.

6. Place the bacon, mushrooms, and peppers in the bottom of a 9-inch / 25-cm square ovenproof dish, and stir in the tomatoes, chile flakes, herbs, salt, and pepper.

7. Layer the spinach over the tomatoes and make 4 wells for the eggs. Drizzle the yogurt over the top and crack the eggs into the holes.

8. Sprinkle the cheese and a little more pepper over the tops and bake for 15–20 minutes, depending on how you like your eggs.

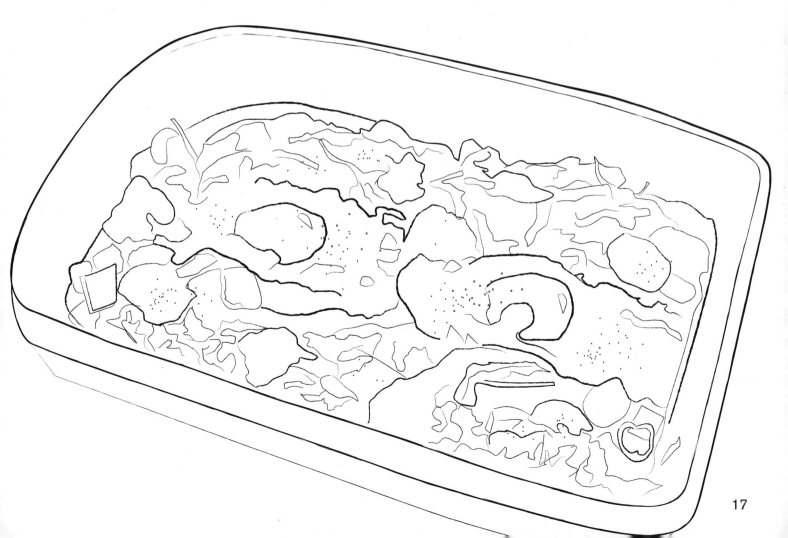

French Toast

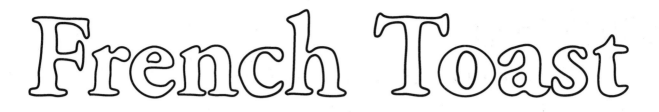

Everyone has a different way of making French toast—the only thing agreed upon is it's the best way to use up stale bread. Thick crusty loaves are perfect, but if you've got some leftover Banana Bread (page 112) then here's a great way of using it up.

Serves 4

You will need:

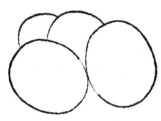

4 large eggs

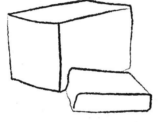

4 tablespoons (2 ounces) / 60 g butter, divided

½ teaspoon salt

2 teaspoons super-fine sugar

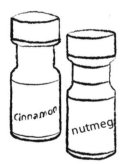

½ teaspoon ground cinnamon

½ teaspoon ground nutmeg

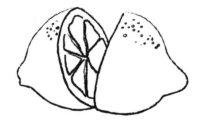

Zest of 1 lemon

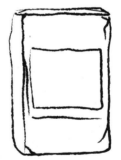

2 tablespoons (1 ounce) / 30 g flour

½ cup (4 ounces) / 125 ml milk

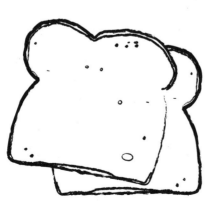

4 thick slices stale, good-quality white bread

Maple syrup, optional

WHaT To Do:

1. Beat the eggs in a wide, shallow bowl.

2. Melt 1 tablespoon of butter and whisk in, along with the salt, sugar, spices, and zest.

3. Add the flour and milk, little by little, to make a paste then beat until smooth.

4. Heat the remaining butter in a frying pan over medium heat, taking care not to let the butter burn.

5. Meanwhile, soak the bread in the egg mixture for about 1 minute, until soft but not falling apart.

6. Place soaked bread in the hot pan and fry for about 2 minutes until golden and crisp—resist the urge to move it; leave it undisturbed. Turn over and fry for about 1 minute more on the other side.

7. Serve with a drizzle of maple syrup or a sprinkling of sugar. Really crispy bacon goes well with this, as does scrambled eggs.

CINNAMON PANCAKES

Once you learn how to make pancakes from scratch you'll never want to buy a packaged mix from the store again; so easy to make and always light and fluffy.

Serves 4

YOU WILL NEED:

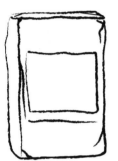

¾ cup (5 ounces) /
140 g all-purpose flour

1 teaspoon
baking powder

2 teaspoons
ground cinnamon

3 tablespoons (1 ½ ounces) /
45 g brown sugar

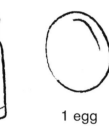

½ teaspoon
salt

1 egg

1 cup (8 ounces) /
250 ml milk

1 teaspoon
vanilla extract

2 tablespoons (1 ounce) /
30 g butter, melted

1 tablespoon canola oil

Toppings of choice such as maple syrup, jelly,
yogurt, fruit, ice cream, or bacon and eggs

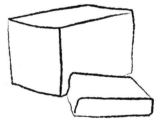

WHAT TO DO:

1. In a large bowl, combine the flour, baking powder, cinnamon, sugar, and salt.

2. In a small bowl, whisk together the egg, milk, vanilla, and butter.

3. Make a well in the center of the flour mixture and slowly pour in the milk mixture, whisking as you go to make a smooth batter free from lumps. You can fry the batter straight away but leaving it to stand for 1 hour or even longer lets the batter thicken and rise.

4. Heat the oil in a nonstick frying pan over medium-high heat. Drop in about 2 tablespoons (1 ounce) / 30 g of the batter to make each pancake. Cook for 2–3 minutes until bubbles appear on the surface (don't move it during this time) then flip over with a spatula and cook for 1 minute more, until golden brown.

5. Serve with your favorite topping.

BLUEBERRY MUFFINS

This is a light version of the classic muffin, with hardly any saturated fat. Make the night before for an excellent weekend breakfast. These will keep for up to 3 days in an airtight container.

Makes 12

You will need:

1 cup (8 ounces) / 225 g self-rising flour

1/2 cup (4 ounces) / 115 g whole-wheat flour

2 teaspoons baking soda

1 teaspoon ground cinnamon

Zest of 1 small orange and 1 teaspoon juice

1/3 cup (3 ounces) / 90 g light brown sugar, divided

1 small very ripe banana

1 large egg

1 1/4 cups (10 ounces) / 310 ml buttermilk

1 teaspoon vanilla extract

1 tablespoon milk

1/2 cup (4 ounces) / 125 ml maple syrup

5 tablespoons (2 1/2 ounces) / 75 ml canola oil

1 cup (8 ounces) / 225 g fresh or frozen blueberries

WHAT TO DO:

1. Preheat oven to 400 degrees F / 200 degrees C / gas mark 6. Place muffin papers in a 12-cup muffin tin.

2. In a large bowl, mix together both flours, baking soda, cinnamon, and orange zest.

3. Set aside 1 tablespoon of the brown sugar for later then stir the rest into the mix.

4. Make a well in the center of the mixture.

5. Mash the banana with a fork.

6. In another bowl, beat the egg then stir in the banana, buttermilk, vanilla, milk, maple syrup, orange juice, and oil. Combine until the oil no longer separates.

7. Using a large metal spoon, very lightly stir wet ingredients into the dry mix just to combine; over-mixing will make the muffins tough.

8. Toss in the blueberries and give just a few turns of the spoon so they're not crushed.

9. Spoon the mixture into the muffin cups, filling each to the top. Sprinkle the rest of the brown sugar over top.

10. Bake for 20 minutes, or until golden. Leave in the tin for 15 minutes to cool a little, as they're very delicate while hot.

Oatmeal chocolate pecan muffins

These are a really satisfying gutsy muffin, but stay surprisingly moist. They go perfectly with a big class of ice-cold milk or a hot cup of coffee or tea.

Makes 12

YOU WILL NEED:

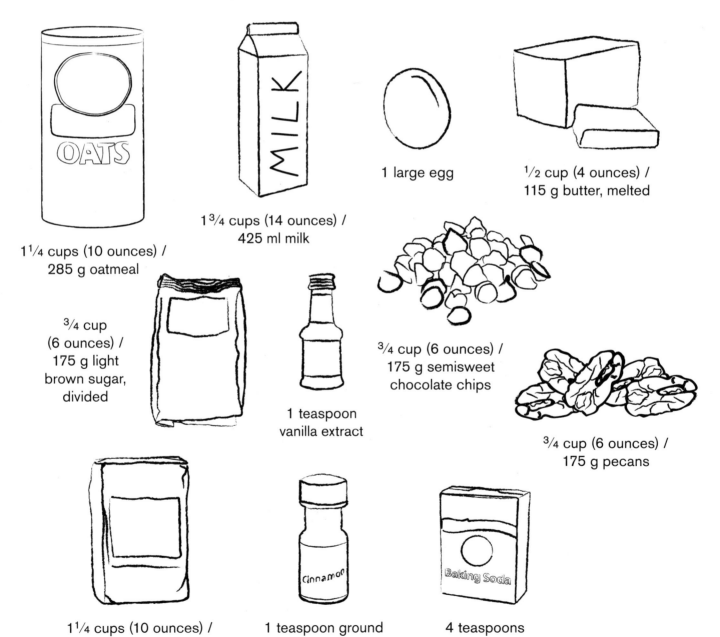

OATS

1¼ cups (10 ounces) / 285 g oatmeal

1 ¾ cups (14 ounces) / 425 ml milk

1 large egg

½ cup (4 ounces) / 115 g butter, melted

¾ cup (6 ounces) / 175 g light brown sugar, divided

1 teaspoon vanilla extract

¾ cup (6 ounces) / 175 g semisweet chocolate chips

¾ cup (6 ounces) / 175 g pecans

1¼ cups (10 ounces) / 285 g whole-wheat flour

Cinnamon

1 teaspoon ground cinnamon

Baking Soda

4 teaspoons baking soda

WHAT TO DO:

1. Preheat oven to 400 degrees F / 200 degrees C / gas mark 6. Place muffin papers in a 12-cup muffin tin.

2. Combine oatmeal and milk in a bowl and soak for 15 minutes.

3. Chop $1/2$ cup (4 ounces) / 115 g of the pecans, leaving the remaining pecans whole.

4. Beat the egg and butter together with $1/2$ cup (4 ounces) / 115 g brown sugar and the vanilla, chocolate chips, and chopped pecans.

5. Stir this into the oat and milk mixture.

6. In a separate bowl, combine the flour, cinnamon, and baking soda. Add this to the oat mixture, stirring until just moist.

7. Fill each muffin cup $3/4$ full. Sprinkle tops with the remaining brown sugar and remaining whole pecans. Bake for 20 minutes until golden.

SALADS AND SIDES

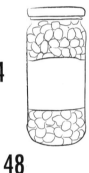

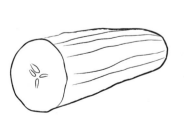

FRUIT SALAD

Colorful and bursting with fresh, juicy fruit, this salad is served with a zesty, gingery syrup which perfectly complements the sugary sweetness.

Serves 6

You will need:

2 oranges

½ cup (3½ ounces) / 115 g super-fine sugar

Zest and juice of 1 lime

1 tablespoon finely grated fresh gingerroot

1 kiwi

8 ounces / 225 g strawberries

8 ounces / 225 g watermelon

1 banana

1 pear

1 Granny Smith apple

1 cup (8 ounces) / 225 g white grapes
1 cup (8 ounces) / 225 g black grapes

½ cup (4 ounces) / 125 g mint leaves

WHaT To Do:

1. Slice 1 orange into segments; set aside.

2. Squeeze the other orange into a measuring cup. Add water until you have $1/2$ cup (4 ounces) / 125 ml liquid.

3. Heat the juice in a small saucepan, adding the sugar until it dissolves, then add the lime zest and ginger. Bring everything to a boil then immediately reduce to a simmer over low heat for 10 minutes. Remove from heat and leave to cool.

4. Chop the strawberries, watermelon, banana, kiwi, pear, and apple into bite-size pieces. You can leave the grapes whole.

5. Combine all the fruit plus the orange segments into a large bowl and squeeze in the lime juice, stirring everything together. The lime helps the fruit keep its color.

6. Once the syrup is completely cool, pour over the fruit and coat completely. Roughly rip the mint leaves and sprinkle over the top. Chill in the refrigerator or serve immediately.

Creamy Potato Salad

An excellent companion to fish or to bring to a barbecue; this can easily be doubled if you're feeding a larger crowd, and can be made the night before and chilled in the refrigerator.

Serves 4

YOU WILL NEED:

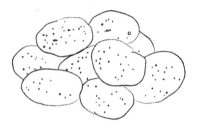

10 ounces / 285 g small potatoes

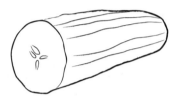

¼ cucumber

3 tablespoons (1 ½ ounces) / 45 g plain yogurt

3 tablespoons (1 ½ ounces) / 45 g mayonnaise

Juice and zest of half a lemon

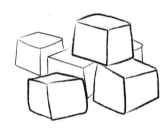

1 cup (8 ounces) / 225 g diced cheddar cheese

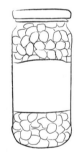

1 tablespoon small capers, rinsed

2 green onions, finely sliced

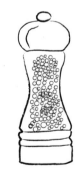

Freshly ground black pepper, to taste

1 teaspoon paprika

WHaT TO DO:

1. Peel the potatoes and cucumber, unless you prefer to leave the skins on. Dice the cucumber and set aside.

2. Cut the potatoes in half and boil in salted water for 15 minutes until just tender. Drain and rinse under cold water to cool then place on paper towels to dry.

3. In a small bowl, mix together the yogurt, mayonnaise, lemon juice, and zest.

4. Place the potatoes into a serving dish and gently stir in the mayonnaise mix, adding the cheese, capers, ¾ of the green onions, and cucumber. Season with pepper and add the paprika. Stir until potatoes are well coated. Top with the remaining green onions and serve.

ITALIAN BEAN AND OLIVE SALAD

Fresh, crunchy, and healthy, the colors in this salad make it perfect for a sunny afternoon. It takes less than 20 minutes to prepare so it can be made just before needed or the night before and kept in the refrigerator.

Serves 6

YOU WILL NEED:

1 red and 1 yellow bell pepper

2 (14-ounce / 400-g) cans mixed beans

1½ cups (12 ounces) / 350 g cherry tomatoes, halved

1 red onion, finely sliced

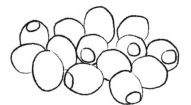

½ cup (4 ounces) / 115 g whole pitted black olives

1 tablespoon small capers

2 tablespoons (1 ounce) / 30 g chopped parsley

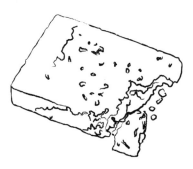

1 cup (8 ounces) / 225 g diced feta cheese

1 tablespoon extra virgin olive oil

2 tablespoons (1 ounce) / 30 g red wine vinegar

Freshly ground black pepper and salt, to taste

WHAT TO DO:

1. Cut the bell peppers into halves and remove seeds. Roast them in a hot oven under the broiler or over an open flame until the skin starts to blister and char then place them into a bowl. Once cool, cut into strips, keeping any juices.

2. Drain the beans and rinse well under cold water to remove any excess brine.

3. Place the drained beans in a large bowl with the bell peppers, tomatoes, onion, olives, capers, and parsley. Stir together, adding the feta.

4. Dress with the oil and vinegar and season with freshly ground black pepper and a pinch of salt. Toss gently to combine. Serve immediately or refrigerate until ready to serve.

RANCH PASTA SALAD

This salad is great as a side dish or as a quick and colorful lunch. Mixing mayonnaise with the ranch dressing makes it really creamy and tasty. Using canned sliced olives saves time but you can switch out with whole olives if you prefer.

Serves 8-10

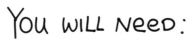

You will need:

1 1/2 cups (12 ounces) /
350 g uncooked farfalle pasta

10 slices bacon

1/2 cup (4 ounces) /
115 g mayonnaise

1 cup (8 ounces) /
225 g ranch dressing

1/2 cup (4 ounces) /
125 ml olive oil

1 (2 1/4-ounce / 50-g) can
sliced black olives, drained

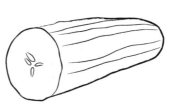

2 cucumbers, diced

1 red onion,
peeled and diced

1 yellow bell pepper,
seeded and diced

1 green bell pepper,
seeded and diced

1 large tomato, diced

Salt and
pepper, to taste

2 tablespoons
(1 ounce) / 30 g grated
Parmesan cheese

WHAT TO DO:

1. Cook pasta according to package directions, rinse in cold water, and drain. Sprinkle with a little oil and toss to keep the pasta from sticking together.

2. Cut bacon into small squares and place in a frying pan over medium-high heat. Fry until evenly brown, but not crispy.

3. In a large bowl, mix together the mayonnaise, ranch dressing, and olive oil.

4. Add the pasta, bacon, olives, cucumbers, onion, bell peppers, and tomato; toss well to coat with the dressing. Season with salt and pepper.

5. Refrigerate for at least 4 hours to give time for flavors to develop. When ready to serve, sprinkle Parmesan cheese over top. Store in the refrigerator for up to 5 days.

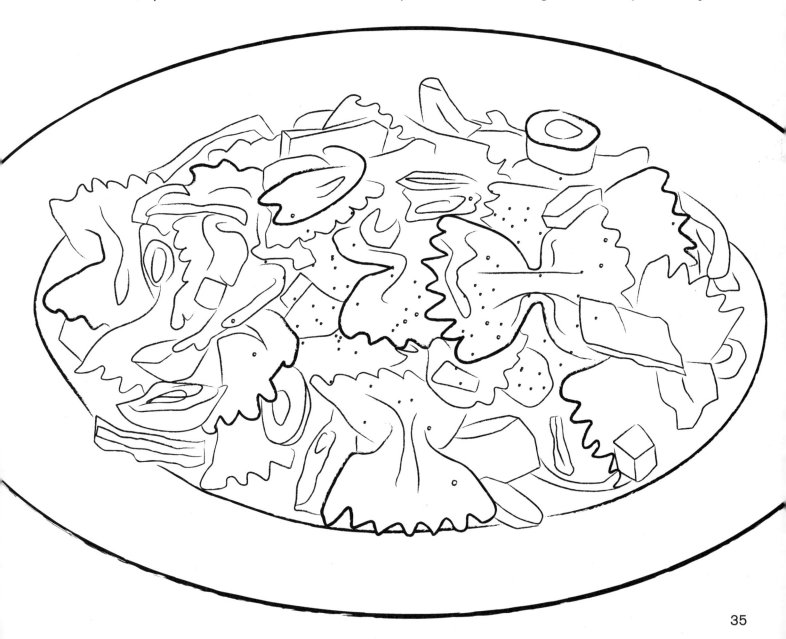

Rainbow Coleslaw

A bright, fun, and colorful coleslaw to liven up any mealtime. The hint of apple and honey gives this a sweet edge, perfect as a side dish with barbecue food. This can be made and eaten immediately, but tastes best if made the day before and kept in the refrigerator overnight.

Serves 8-10   YOU WILL NEED:

2 cups (16 ounces) / 500 g mayonnaise

2 tablespoons (1 ounce) / 30 ml apple cider vinegar

¼ cup (2 ounces) / 60 ml lemon juice

1 teaspoon ground cumin

¼ cup (2 ounces) / 60 ml honey or maple syrup

1 tablespoon olive oil

Salt and pepper, to taste

1 red bell pepper
1 yellow bell pepper

1 cup (8 ounces) / 225 g sugar snap peas

4 green onions

½ pound / 225 g carrots

1 large unpeeled apple, cored

1 pound / 450 g red cabbage

½ pound / 225 g green cabbage

2 teaspoons paprika

1 cup (8 ounces) / 225 g cilantro, chopped

36

WHAT TO DO:

1. In a small bowl, mix together the mayonnaise, vinegar, lemon juice, cumin, and honey until well combined. Slowly stir in the oil, add salt and pepper, and set aside.

2. Cut the bell peppers, snap peas, and green onions into 1-inch slices.

3. Using the large holes on a grater, grate the cabbages, carrots, and apple.

4. Place all the vegetables into a very large bowl. Pour dressing over top and toss until well coated. Cover and chill for at least 1 hour. When ready to serve, sprinkle with the paprika and chopped cilantro.

SALMON AND AVOCADO SALAD

Whether you use smoked or fillets of salmon, this fresh and light salad is served with a zesty dressing and a base of avocado and cucumber; a perfect summery lunchtime meal.

Serves 4

You will need:

2 tablespoons (1 ounce) / 30 g pine nuts

12 ounces / 350 g smoked salmon or 4 small salmon fillets

3 tablespoons (1 1/2 ounces) / 45 ml olive oil, divided

Salt and pepper, to taste

2 teaspoons honey

2 tablespoons (1 ounce) / 30 ml freshly squeezed lemon juice

1 3/4 cups (14 ounces) / 425 g mixed salad greens

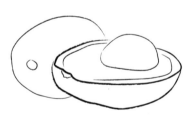

2 small avocados

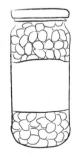

2 tablespoons (1 ounce) / 30 g capers

1/2 cucumber

1 cup (8 ounces) / 225 g combined fresh basil and fresh dill

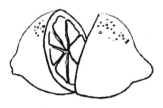

1 lemon, cut into wedges

WHAT TO DO:

1. Lightly toast the pine nuts in a dry pan over medium–low heat; set aside to cool.

2. If using salmon fillets, use the same pan on the same heat. Season the fillets with 1 tablespoon oil and salt and pepper. Place in the pan and fry for 3–4 minutes on each side. Remove from heat to cool and then flake into pieces. If using smoked salmon, remove from refrigerator and flake into pieces; set aside.

3. In a small bowl, stir together the remaining oil, honey, and lemon juice, and season with salt and pepper.

4. Arrange the salad greens on 4 serving plates, leaving room in the center.

5. Remove the pit from the avocados and slice. Evenly divide the slices and place in the center of the salad leaves with a scattering of capers.

6. Using a potato peeler, slice the cucumber into long, thin strips and place over top of the avocado. Shred the basil and dill and scatter over the top.

7. Place the salmon on next, drizzle the dressing generously over all 4 plates, and very lightly toss everything together. Lastly, add the toasted pine nuts and serve with lemon wedges.

Corn and Zucchini Sauté

Whether you use fresh from the cob, canned, or frozen sweet corn, this speedy side dish is bright, colorful, and tasty.

Serves 6

 You will need:

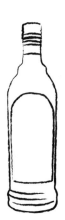

2 tablespoons
(1 ounce) / 30 ml olive oil

1 medium white onion,
peeled and diced

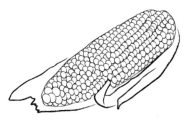

1 medium red bell pepper,
seeded and diced

1 clove garlic, peeled
and minced

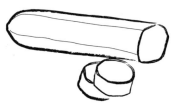

1 pound / 450 g zucchini

1 pound / 450 g corn kernels

1/2 cup (4 ounces) / 115 g
chopped fresh cilantro

Salt and pepper,
to taste

1 teaspoon lemon juice

40

WHAT TO DO:

1. Heat oil in a large frying pan over medium heat and add the onion, stirring occasionally, for about 5 minutes.

2. Add the bell pepper and continue sautéing for 5 minutes until softened then add the garlic and stir together over the heat for 1 minute.

3. Cut the zucchini into thick slices and quarter each section. Add to the pan with the corn, and cook for around 5 minutes.

4. Remove from the heat, stir in the cilantro, salt, pepper, and the lemon juice and serve immediately.

LEMON AND GARLIC ROASTED BROCCOLI

Turn this simple green vegetable into something no one will want to leave on their plate; a hint of chile and lemon give this a refreshing, tangy finish.

Serves 6

You will need:

2 tablespoons
(1 ounce) /
30 ml olive oil

2 cloves garlic,
peeled and minced

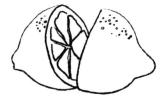

Zest and juice of
1 small lemon

Salt and pepper,
to taste

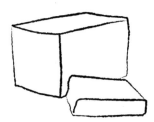

2 tablespoons (1 ounce) /
30 g unsalted butter

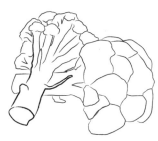

1 pound / 450 g
broccoli florets

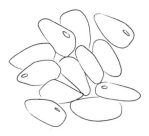

2 tablespoons (1 ounce) /
30 g pine nuts

¼ teaspoon dried
chile flakes

WHAT TO DO:

1. Preheat oven to 400 degrees F / 200 degrees C / gas mark 6.

2. In a large saucepan, heat the oil over medium-low heat. Add the garlic and zest and sauté for about 1 minute; don't let it get too hot and burn.

3. Remove from heat and melt in the butter as it cools.

4. Stir in 1 tablespoon of the lemon juice. Season with salt and pepper.

5. Separate the broccoli into florets and add to the saucepan along with the pine nuts and chile flakes; stir everything together to coat.

6. Arrange the florets on a baking sheet and roast for 15–20 minutes, until tender. Transfer to a serving plate or bowl, and sprinkle remaining lemon juice over the top.

SWEET AND SAVORY KALE

Kale, when uncooked, can be quite tough and earthy; add a sweet and savory twist to this nutritious green. If you plan to serve as a side dish, you can omit the avocado and cheese, otherwise this makes a wonderful warm evening salad.

Serves 6

YOU WILL NEED:

1 small red
onion, diced

2 cloves garlic,
peeled and minced

1 tablespoon
Dijon mustard

2 tablespoons
(1 ounce) / 30 ml
honey or maple syrup

2 tablespoons
(1 ounce) /
30 ml canola oil

1 tablespoon apple
cider vinegar

1 1/2 cups (12 ounces) /
375 ml chicken stock

2 pounds / 900 g kale

1/4 cup (2 ounces) /
60 g dried cranberries

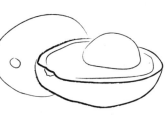
1 small avocado

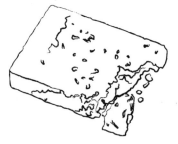
1/2 cup (4 ounces) /
115 g feta or Brie cheese

1/4 cup (2 ounces) /
60 g sliced almonds

What to do:

1. Heat the oil in a large pot over medium heat.

2. Stir in the onion, cook until it softens and turns translucent, and then add the garlic and stir together for 1 minute.

3. Add the mustard, honey, vinegar, and stock; turn the heat up to high and bring to a boil.

4. Stem, rinse, and tear the kale into smaller pieces and add to the pot along with the dried cranberries. Cover with a lid and turn the heat back to medium and simmer for 5 minutes until wilted. Then remove the lid and continue to cook until the liquid has reduced by about half; about 10 minutes.

5. While the kale and cranberries are cooking, cube the avocado and feta.

6. Remove the kale from the heat, drain if necessary, and toss together with the avocado and cheese. Sprinkle with almonds and serve immediately.

LEMONY SNAP PEAS

The combination of crisp snap peas and cucumber with fresh lemon juice and olive oil makes a refreshing side dish for late summer evening meals.

Serves 4

1 1/2 cups (12 ounces) / 350 g sugar snap peas, trimmed

1 small cucumber

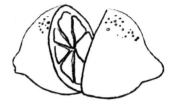

Juice and zest of 1 large lemon

1 tablespoon extra virgin olive oil

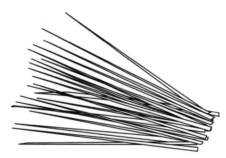

3 tablespoons (1 1/2 ounces) / 45 g chopped fresh chives

1 teaspoon Dijon mustard

1 teaspoon sugar

Pinch of sea salt

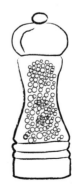

Pinch of black pepper

WHɘT TO DO:

1. Place the peas in a large saucepan of boiling water and cook for 1 minute. Drain immediately and place into an ice-water bath to stop the cooking process; drain. Slice some of the peas lengthways to reveal the peas inside.

2. Cut the cucumber in half, and using a potato peeler, shave off thin slices (include the skin if desired) until all the cucumber is cut in this way.

3. Add the lemon juice, zest, and remaining ingredients to a medium bowl; stir to combine.

4. Stir the peas and cucumber shavings into the dressing. Serve immediately.

SIZZLED ONIONS AND PEPPERS

Something so simple shouldn't be as tasty as this. Serve over steak, in a chicken wrap, or with barbecue sausages on a hot summer day.

Serves 4

You WILL NEED:

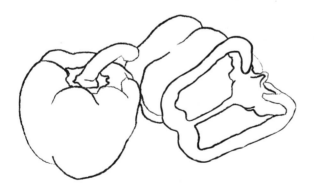

2 tablespoons (1 ounce) / 30 g olive oil

3 large red onions

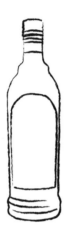

3 mixed bell peppers, any color

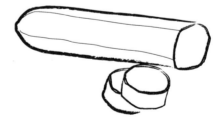

1 zucchini, optional

1 clove garlic, crushed, optional

1 teaspoon smoked paprika

WHAT TO DO:

1. Heat the oil in a large frying pan over high heat or directly on the barbecue grill.

2. Chop the onions into wedges and slice the bell peppers into fairly large pieces and sauté, stirring frequently.

3. Add the zucchini and garlic, if using.

4. When the vegetables start to soften and turn brown, stir in the paprika. Cook until everything is sizzling and hot then serve.

New Potatoes with Bacon

Turn run-of-the-mill new potatoes into something extra special. Take your time frying the potatoes—the crispier, the better.

Serves 4

YOU WILL NEED:

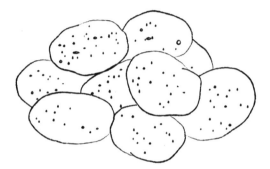

16 new potatoes, roughly chopped

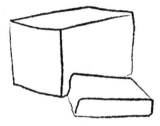

4 tablespoons
(2 ounces) / 60 g butter

4 tablespoons (2 ounces) /
60 g canola oil

2 small white
onions, sliced

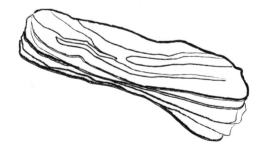

6 slices bacon, cut into squares

Salt, to taste

WHAT TO DO:

1. Boil potatoes in salted water for 5–10 minutes or until tender.

2. Heat a large frying pan over medium heat. Add the butter and oil. Fry the onions and bacon until crispy and browned.

3. Drain the potatoes, add salt, and add to the frying pan with the bacon and onions. Fry for 5–10 minutes until golden and crisp. Serve immediately.

SWEET POTATO FRIES

These beat normal fries hands down. Cut them big and chunky; the salt and seasoning really brings out the sweetness of the potatoes.

Serves 8

You will need:

4 large sweet potatoes

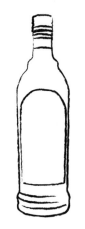

2–3 tablespoons
(1–1 1/2 ounces) /
30–45 g olive oil

2 tablespoons
(1 ounce) / 30 g sea salt

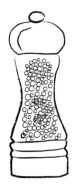

Freshly ground
black pepper

1 teaspoon sugar

1 tablespoon sweet
smoked paprika

1 tablespoon
mixed dried herbs

1 teaspoon dried
chile flakes

WHAT TO DO:

1. Preheat oven to 400 degrees F / 200 degrees C / gas mark 6.

2. Wash the potatoes under cold running water; leave the skins on. Cut each potato in half lengthways then cut each half lengthways, so you get roughly 8–10 wedges from each potato. Don't worry about being exact. Add to a large bowl.

3. Drizzle oil over wedges then add the salt, pepper, sugar, paprika, herbs, and chile flakes. Stir well so all the potato pieces are coated.

4. Spread out as a single layer on a large baking sheet (you may need two) and bake for 35–40 minutes, or until the potatoes are really crispy and golden. When they're done, let them rest for a couple of minutes, so they don't fall apart when you remove them from the baking sheet.

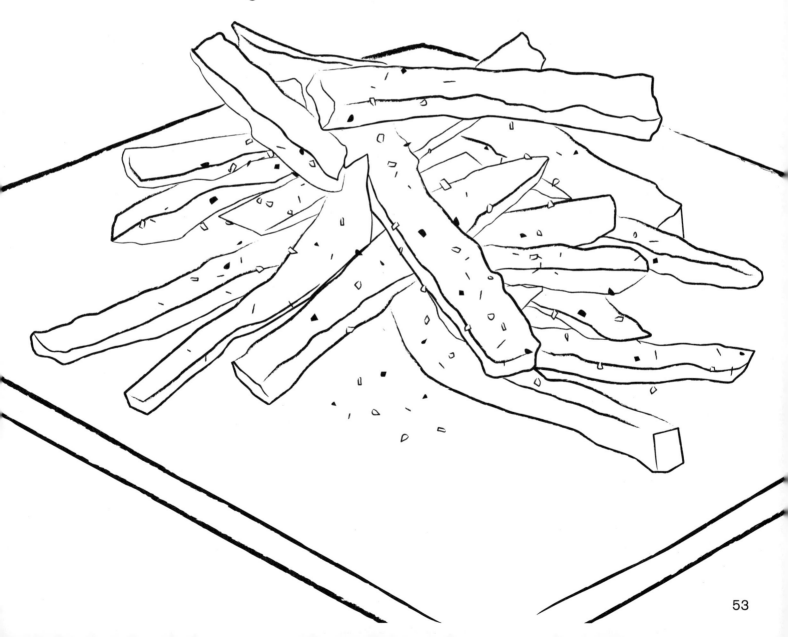

Spicy Rice

Add a bit of kick to a mostly overlooked side dish; you can even add peas and leftover chicken to make it more substantial.

Serves 4

You will need:

3 tablespoons
(1 1/2 ounces) /
45 g vegetable oil

1 white onion,
finely chopped

1 cup (8 ounces) /
225 g uncooked rice

1/2 cup (4 ounces) / 125 ml
hot vegetable stock

1 teaspoon chili
powder, or to taste

1 teaspoon turmeric

1 teaspoon salt

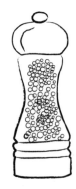

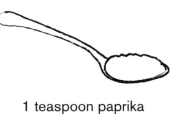

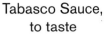

Freshly ground
pepper, to taste

Tabasco Sauce,
to taste

1 teaspoon paprika

1/2 teaspoon
cumin seeds

WHAT TO DO:

1. Heat the oil in a large pan and sauté the onion until golden brown.

2. Fry the rice with the oil and onion for 3–4 minutes, stirring frequently. When the rice starts to brown slightly, add the stock and chili powder; add more if you like it really spicy.

3. Add the turmeric and simmer for 15 minutes until the water begins to be absorbed.

4. Now add the salt, pepper, Tabasco, paprika, and cumin. Keep stirring until everything is absorbed and the rice is fluffy and cooked through, adding more boiling water if necessary.

CREAMY RISOTTO

Risotto is a perfect vehicle for all kinds of wonderful ingredients. If you have leftover vegetables or sausages that need using up, you can create a really tasty dish with whatever you have. Alternatively you can keep it simple and creamy with just a few ingredients.

Serves 4

YOU WILL NEED:

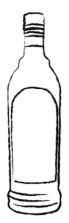

2 tablespoons
(1 ounce) / 30 ml olive oil

1 large white onion,
peeled and diced

4 cloves garlic, peeled

1 ¾ cups
(14 ounces) / 410 g
risotto (Arborio) rice

4 tablespoons
(2 ounces) / 60 ml heavy
cream or crème fraîche

1 cup (4 ounces) / 115 g
grated cheddar cheese

3 cups (24 ounces) /
750 ml hot vegetable stock

3 tablespoons
(1 ½ ounces) / 45 g
grated Parmesan
cheese, divided

Freshly ground black
pepper, to taste

Optional add-ins:
Vegetables such as zucchini, bell peppers,
mushrooms, broccoli, sugar snap peas, spinach
Chicken, sausages, salmon, any choice of meat

WHAT TO DO:

1. Heat the oil in a large pot; add the onions and garlic and sauté over low heat until they begin to soften. If you are adding additional vegetables or meats, chop and add at this stage. If you choose not to include anything additional then move to the next step.

2. Stir the vegetables until browned.

3. Add the rice and stir to coat with the oil, for about 2 minutes.

4. Slowly add the stock $1/2$ cup (4 ounces) / 118 ml at a time, stirring constantly. When the rice has soaked up the liquid, add more. Repeat for around 20–30 minutes until all the stock has been used. Taste the rice to ensure it is soft and not still hard inside. If you need to, add more boiling water until the rice is fully cooked.

5. Stir in the cream until well mixed, and then stir in the cheddar cheese until fully melted. Add the Parmesan, reserving 1 tablespoon. Season with plenty of black pepper.

6. If you choose, you can also wilt in some spinach before serving. Ladle onto plates and sprinkle with the remaining Parmesan to serve.

MAIN COURSES

Tomato Soup

This is a versatile and handy soup to have in your repertoire; serve as an appetizer, a lunch, or a main dish with plenty of crusty bread.

Serves 4

You will need:

2 pounds / 900 g
ripe tomatoes

2 medium yellow onions

1 small carrot

1 stalk celery

2 cloves garlic, crushed

2 teaspoons tomato paste

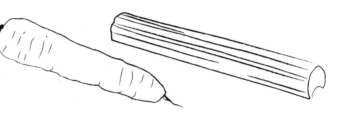

Pinch of sugar

2 tablespoons
(1 ounce) /
30 ml olive oil

Salt and pepper,
to taste

2 bay leaves

1 (14-ounce / 400-g)
can chopped tomatoes

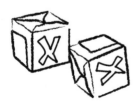

2 bouillon cubes,
beef or chicken

4¼ cups (34 ounces) /
1 l hot water

5 tablespoons (2½ ounces) /
75 g sour cream

1 handful of fresh
basil leaves

WHƏT TO DO:

1. Cut the tomatoes into quarters, removing any hard cores; set aside.

2. Chop the onions, carrot, and celery into small pieces and place in a large pot. Sauté in oil over medium heat until soft and faintly colored.

3. Add garlic and tomato paste and stir well to coat vegetables. Add the tomatoes and season with the sugar, salt, and pepper.

4. Tear bay leaves into a few pieces and add along with canned tomatoes. Stir everything together, cover with lid, and simmer over a low heat for 10 minutes.

5. Combine the bouillon cubes with the water to make a stock, and slowly add to pot, stirring as you go. Turn the heat up to high and boil for 2 minutes then turn the heat down to low again and replace the lid. Cook gently for 25 minutes, stirring every so often.

6. Remove the pot from the heat then find the pieces of bay leaf and discard.

7. Pour the soup into a blender or food processor (use a ladle) until it is ¾ full then blend for about 30 seconds. Pour this puréed soup into a large bowl. Repeat until you have blended everything to a consistency you like.

8. Pour the puréed soup back into the pot and reheat it over a medium heat for a few minutes. Stir in the sour cream and add more seasoning, if necessary.

9. Ladle into bowls, top with the basil leaves, and serve.

Homemade Pizza

If you think making pizza at home involves hours of kneading dough, think again. This frying pan version, with its thin and crispy base and roasted toppings, is easy to make and super tasty.

Serves 4

YOU WILL NEED:

1 yellow bell pepper, seeded and cut into chunks

1 zucchini, cut into chunks

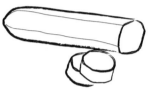

1 red onion, peeled and cut into wedges

2 tablespoons (1 ounce) / 30 ml canola oil, plus 1 teaspoon, divided

Sea salt, to taste

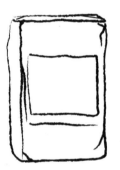

1 cup (8 ounces) / 225 g self-rising flour

4–5 tablespoons / 60–75 ml water

1 (14-ounce / 400-g) can chopped tomatoes, divided

1 handful fresh basil leaves

½ clove garlic, peeled

1 teaspoon balsamic vinegar

2 ounces / 50 g mozzarella cheese, sliced

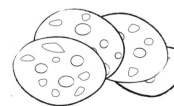

8 slices salami

WHat to Do:

1. Preheat oven to 425 degrees F / 220 degrees C / gas mark 7.

2. Place the bell pepper, zucchini, and onion on a large nonstick baking sheet and cover evenly with 1 teaspoon of oil and a good sprinkling of salt. Roast in the oven for 20 minutes, remove, and set aside.

3. Heat the broiler / grill to medium.

4. In a large bowl, mix the flour with the remaining oil and water to form a soft dough. Knead briefly then roll out on a floured surface to a rough 8-inch / 20-cm circle.

5. Transfer the dough to a large ovenproof, nonstick frying pan and fry over medium heat for 5 minutes, until the underside begins to brown. Turn dough over and cook for 5 minutes until bottom starts to brown; remove from heat.

6. Place $\frac{1}{3}$ of the chopped tomatoes into a blender with the basil, garlic, balsamic vinegar, and a pinch of salt. Blend until smooth.

7. Pour the sauce over the middle of the pizza crust and spread out evenly. Top with mozzarella slices, roasted vegetables, and salami. Place the pan directly under the broiler / grill for 3–4 minutes, or until the cheese has melted. Serve immediately.

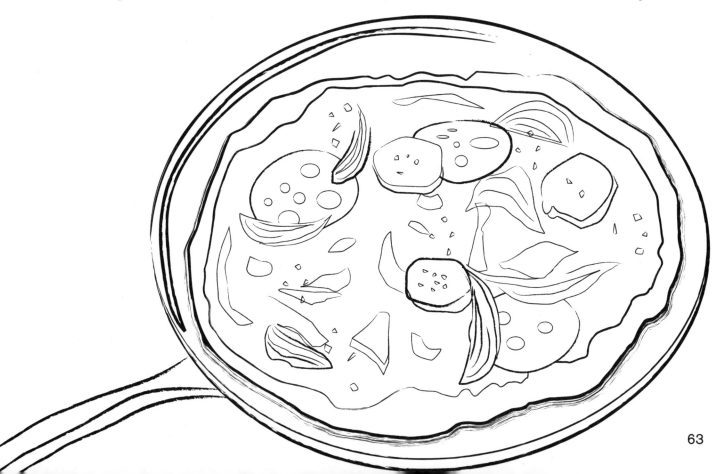

STUFFED PEPPERS

A quick and simple mid-week dish; minimal preparation and great for vegetarians, too.

Serves 4

You will need:

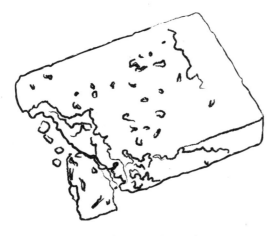

4 large bell peppers, any color of choice, seeded and cut in half lengthwise

1/2 cup (4 ounces) / 115 ml boiling water

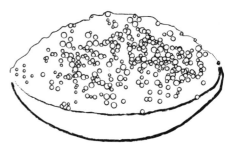

3/4 cup (6 ounces) / 175 g couscous

1/4 cup (2 ounces) / 60 g pine nuts, toasted

1 cup (8 ounces) / 225 g black olives, roughly chopped

2 teaspoons dried basil

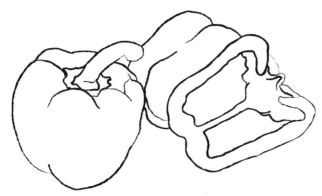

4 ounces / 115 g feta cheese

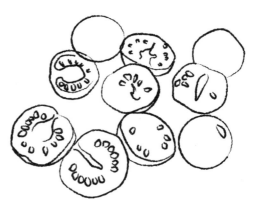

1 cup (8 ounces) / 225 g cherry tomatoes, halved

WHAT TO DO:

1. Preheat oven to 400 degrees F / 200 degrees C / gas mark 6.

2. Put the bell peppers in the microwave on medium power for 5 minutes, until just soft. Place on a baking sheet, cut-side up.

3. In a bowl, pour boiling water over the couscous. Stir, cover the bowl, and let stand for 10 minutes.

4. Stir the couscous with a fork to break it up then mix in the pine nuts, olives, basil, feta, and tomatoes. Stuff the pepper halves with the couscous mixture and bake for 10 minutes. Serve.

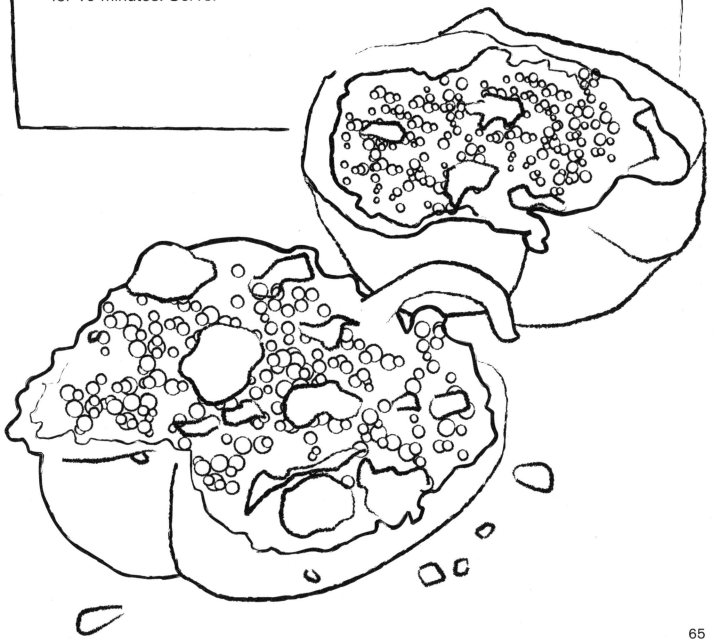

Meatloaf

Meatloaf is the archetypal American meal. Full of nostalgia, it is easy and delicious, too. This recipe uses turkey as a low-fat alternative to beef. By adding a tangy and sweet barbecue glaze, there's still a lot of flavor to be found here. Try serving in a sandwich with lots of creamy mayonnaise.

Serves 6

YOU WILL NEED:

2 slices slightly stale bread

2 tablespoons (1 ounce) / 30 g butter

1 yellow onion, diced

3 cloves garlic, minced

1¼ pounds / 560 g ground turkey

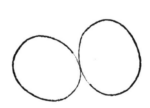
2 eggs, beaten

2 tablespoons (1 ounce) / 30 g paprika

Salt and pepper, to taste

2 cups (16 ounces) / 500 ml tomato sauce, divided

2 tablespoons (1 ounce) / 30 g Dijon mustard

2 tablespoons (1 ounce) / 30 ml Worcestershire sauce

3 tablespoons (1½ ounces) / 45 g brown sugar

3 tablespoons (1½ ounces) / 45 ml vinegar

WHAT TO DO:

1. Preheat oven to 350 degrees F / 180 degrees C / gas mark 4.

2. Make the breadcrumbs by putting the slices of bread in your food processor and grinding into crumbs. You should have around ²/₃ cup / 170 g of crumbs.

3. Melt the butter in a saucepan; add the onion and garlic and sauté over low heat for 5 minutes until softened. Remove from heat and let cool.

4. In a large bowl, mix together the ground turkey, breadcrumbs, eggs, paprika, salt, pepper, ¹/₂ cup (4 ounces) / 110 g tomato sauce, and the cooled onions and garlic.

5. Press mixture into a loaf pan.

6. Stir together the rest of the tomato sauce with the mustard, Worcestershire sauce, brown sugar, and vinegar. Add a little water if it seems too thick.

7. Pour the sauce over the meatloaf, and bake for 1 hour. Leave to stand for 5 minutes before serving.

TUNA PASTA BAKE

This was my favorite childhood dinner growing up; adding chips on top will always remind me of my mum and her amazing ways of adding fun things to normal meals. Ultimate comfort food.

Serves 4

YOU WILL NEED:

2 tablespoons (1 ounce) / 30 ml olive oil

2 red onions, sliced

1 red bell pepper, sliced

2 cloves garlic, minced

1 (6-ounce / 170-g) can water-packed tuna, drained

1 (14-ounce / 400-g) can chopped tomatoes

1 tablespoon capers

1 tablespoon dried mixed herbs

Salt and pepper, to taste

1¼ cups (11 ounces) / 300 g dried pasta of choice

1 (1-ounce / 30-g) bag salted potato chips, crushed

½ cup (2 ounces) / 60 g grated sharp cheddar cheese

½ tablespoon grated Parmesan cheese

WHAT TO DO:

1. Preheat the oven to 350 degrees F / 180 degrees C / gas mark 4.

2. Heat the oil in a large frying pan over medium heat and add the onions, bell pepper, and garlic and cook and stir for around 10 minutes until they start to brown.

3. Add the tuna to the vegetables, stirring for 30 seconds, before pouring in the chopped tomatoes. Add the capers, herbs, and seasoning and simmer for 10 minutes.

4. Place the pasta in a pot of boiling water and start to cook according to package instructions. Only boil for half the required time; the pasta will absorb the rest of the liquid and finish cooking once in the oven—otherwise the pasta overcooks and falls apart.

5. Drain the almost-cooked pasta and add to the pan of tuna. Mix everything together then pour into a 9 x 9-inch / 25 x 25-cm ovenproof dish.

6. Mix together the crushed chips and cheddar cheese and sprinkle over the top of the tuna layer. Season with pepper and a sprinkling of Parmesan.

7. Bake for 20–30 minutes, or until the cheese is bubbling and crispy. Serve with a green salad.

Macaroni and Cheese

An old classic, and fast, too. Everyone has a different version of this, but the two most important things are the ground nutmeg and lots and lots of cheese!

Serves 4

You will need:

3 cups (24 ounces) /
750 ml whole milk

1 white onion, peeled
and halved

1 clove garlic, peeled

1 teaspoon
ground nutmeg

1½ cups (12 ounces) /
350 g macaroni noodles

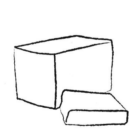

¼ cup (2 ounces) /
60 g butter, plus a little
extra for greasing

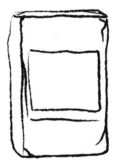

¼ cup (2 ounces) /
60 g flour

1¾ cups (7 ounces)
200 g grated sharp
cheddar cheese

1 teaspoon Dijon mustard

Ground black
pepper, to taste

1 (1-ounce / 30-g) bag
salted potato chips

½ cup (2 ounces) / 60 g
grated Parmesan cheese

WHaT TO DO:

1. Preheat oven to 375 degrees F / 190 C / gas mark 5 and grease a 9 x 7-inch / 25 x 18-cm ovenproof dish.

2. In a small saucepan, heat the milk, onion, garlic, and nutmeg until almost boiling. Remove from heat, cover with a lid, and let infuse for 10 minutes then strain.

3. Cook the macaroni according to package directions, drain, and set aside.

4. Melt the butter in a medium saucepan. Add the flour and stir constantly for 1 minute over low heat.

5. Slowly stir in the infused milk until smooth. Simmer for 5 minutes, or until the sauce has thickened.

6. Remove from heat and stir in the cheddar cheese and mustard. Season with the pepper and stir until all the cheese has melted. Pour the sauce over the cooked macaroni, coating evenly, then tip into the prepared dish.

7. Crush the bag of chips until the contents are completely smashed up then sprinkle on top with the Parmesan—this gives it a really crunchy topping.

8. Bake for 20 minutes until golden and bubbling.

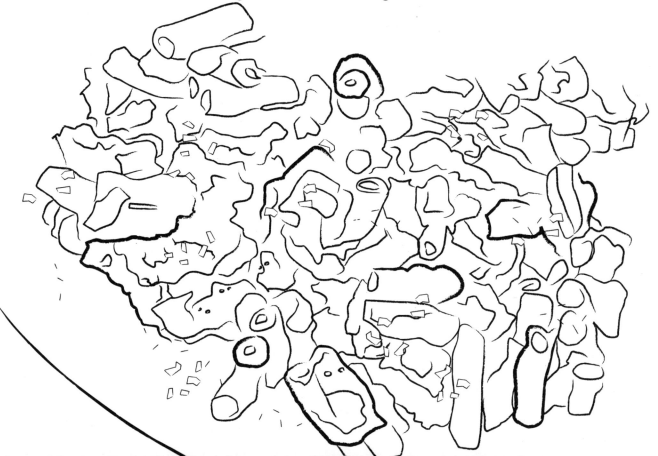

Mediterranean Vegetable Pasta

An easy, fast, and healthy pasta–perfect for summer evenings. Roasting the vegetables gives a great charbroiled flavor.

Serves 4

You will need:

2 red bell peppers, seeded and cut into chunks

2 red onions, cut into wedges

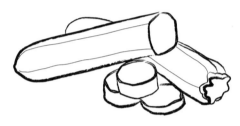

2 medium zucchini, cut into chunks

3 cloves garlic, peeled

2 pounds / 900 g small ripe tomatoes, halved

2 teaspoons sea salt

2 tablespoons (1 ounce) / 30 ml olive oil

1 tablespoon balsamic vinegar

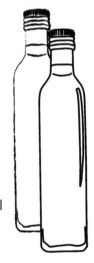

½ cup (4 ounces) / 115 g whole pitted black olives

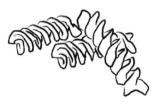

2½ cups (22 ounces) / 600 g dried pasta of choice (fusilli works well)

1 handful of fresh basil leaves

2 tablespoons (1 ounce) / 30 g grated Parmesan cheese

WHAT TO DO:

1. Preheat oven to 400 degrees F / 200 degrees C / gas mark 6.

2. Place the bell peppers, onions, zucchini, garlic, and tomatoes in a large roasting pan. Sprinkle liberally with salt and drizzle the oil and vinegar evenly over the top.

3. Roast for 15 minutes; stir and add the olives.

4. Roast for another 15 minutes, or until everything is softened and the juices run together.

5. While the vegetables are roasting, cook the pasta, according to package directions, in a large pot of salted boiling water. Drain well.

6. Remove the vegetables from the oven, stir in the pasta, and toss lightly together. Tear the basil leaves and sprinkle over top along with the Parmesan.

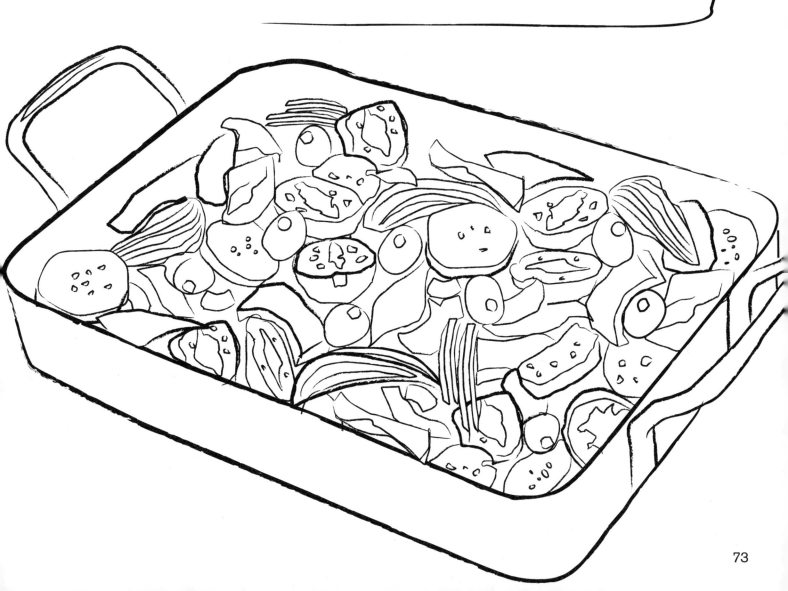

SPAGHETTI BOLOGNESE

Everyone's favorite classic Italian dish—perfect for slurping noodles.

Serves 4

YOU WILL NEED:

2 tablespoons
(1 ounce) /
30 ml olive oil

2 red onions, diced

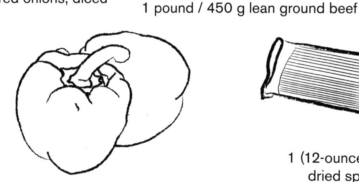

1 pound / 450 g lean ground beef

2 cloves garlic,
peeled and chopped

2 red bell peppers, seeded and diced

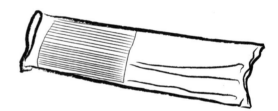

1 (12-ounce / 350-g) package
dried spaghetti noodles

1 (14-ounce /
400-g) can
chopped tomatoes

1 tablespoon
tomato paste

2 teaspoons dried
mixed herbs of choice

Salt and pepper,
to taste

1 teaspoon sugar

1 tablespoon
balsamic vinegar

1 handful fresh basil leaves

2 tablespoons (1 ounce) /
30 g grated Parmesan cheese

WHAT TO DO:

1. Heat the oil in a large pan over medium heat and sauté the onions until translucent. Add the beef and cook until brown.

2. Drain the excess grease off and then add the garlic and bell peppers, cooking until soft.

3. Cook spaghetti noodles according to package directions; drain and set aside.

4. Add the chopped tomatoes, tomato paste, dried herbs, salt, pepper, and sugar to the cooked beef, and bring to boil for 5 minutes.

5. Turn heat down and add the vinegar. Simmer for 15 minutes.

6. Tear up the basil leaves and stir gently through.

7. Add the spaghetti and toss to coat. The authentic way to serve Bolognese is with the sauce coating the pasta, rather than served on top.

LASAGNA

Not as complicated as it seems; it's all about building the layers. Lasagna is perfect when you've got lots of friends for dinner. Serve with a fresh green salad.

Serves 8-10

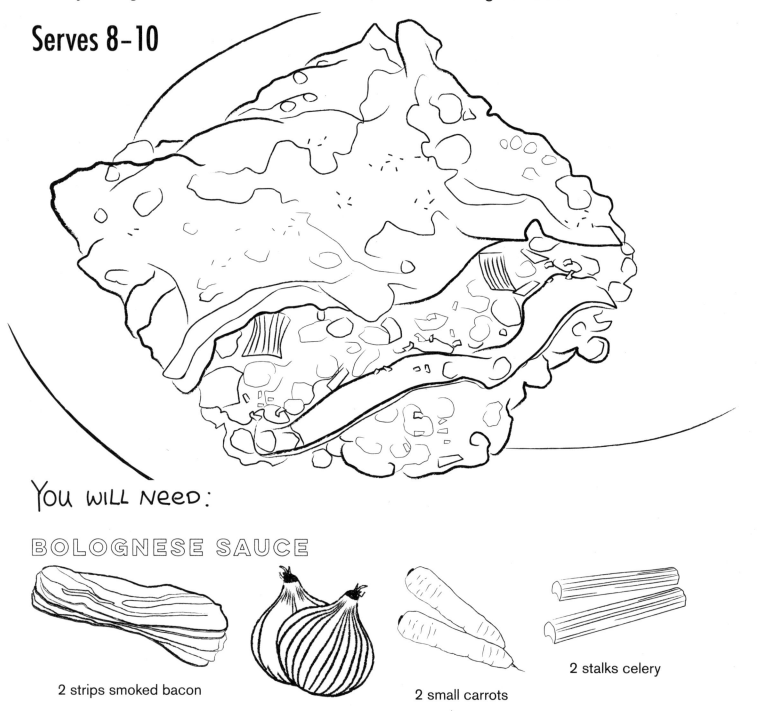

YOU WILL NEED:

BOLOGNESE SAUCE

2 strips smoked bacon

2 medium red onions

2 small carrots

2 stalks celery

2 tablespoons
(1 ounce) /
30 ml canola oil

1 tablespoon
dried oregano

2 cloves garlic,
minced

1 pound / 450 g
good-quality lean ground beef

2 (14-ounce / 400-g)
cans chopped tomatoes

1 ¾ cups (14 ounces) /
425 ml beef stock

Sea salt, to taste

Freshly ground
black pepper

WHITE SAUCE

1 small white onion

2 cups (16 ounces) /
500 ml milk

1 sprig fresh parsley

Pinch of
nutmeg

6 black
peppercorns

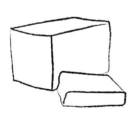

3 tablespoons
(1 ½ ounces) /
45 g butter

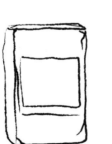

½ cup (4 ounces) /
100 g flour

½ cup (2 ounces) /
60 g grated
cheddar cheese

3 tablespoons (1 ½ ounces) /
45 g grated Parmesan cheese

12 dried lasagna noodles

WHAT TO DO:

BOLOGNESE SAUCE

1. Chop the bacon, onions, carrots, and celery into pieces the about same size.

2. Add the oil to a large saucepan over high heat and cook the bacon with the oregano until lightly golden.

3. Reduce heat to medium low and add the vegetables and the garlic to the pan, stirring occasionally. When vegetables are softened, add the ground beef, brown for 5 minutes, and then add the tomatoes.

4. Add the beef stock to the vegetables with a good pinch of salt and pepper. Stir everything well and bring to boil for 2 minutes. Turn the heat to low and simmer, covered, for 1 hour, stirring occasionally. Add water if it begins to look dry.

WHITE SAUCE

1. Peel and slice the onion and place in a medium saucepan along with the milk, parsley, nutmeg, and peppercorns. Gently bring to a boil, over medium heat, keeping a close eye on the milk so it doesn't boil over or scorch on the bottom of the pan.

2. Strain the milk through a sieve.

3. Melt the butter in a separate pan over low heat then mix in the flour. Slowly add the milk, a bit at a time, stirring continually to prevent lumps. When the sauce is smooth, bring it to a boil and let simmer for a couple of minutes.

4. Remove from heat and add the cheddar cheese; stir until melted.

1. Preheat oven to 375 degrees F / 190 degrees C / gas mark 5.

2. Remove the Bolognese from the heat and spoon 1/3 of it into a 9 x 14-inch / 25 x 35-cm ovenproof dish. Follow with a layer of lasagna noodles; snapping them if necessary to completely cover, and then spoon over a third of the White Sauce.

3. Repeat the process two more times, finishing with a layer of White Sauce; sprinkle Parmesan cheese over top.

4. Cover with aluminum foil and bake for 30 minutes. Remove the foil and bake for 20 minutes more or until the top is golden.

Chicken Parmigiana

A sure-fire crowd pleaser, and deceptively easy. The only hard part is pummeling the chicken, but the end result is well worth the exertion.

Serves 6

You will need:

6 skinless, boneless
chicken breasts

1/2 cup (4 ounces) /
115 g flour

Salt and pepper,
to taste

1 cup (4 ounces) / 115 g
freshly grated Parmesan
cheese, divided

3 eggs, beaten

1/2 cup (4 ounces) /
125 ml olive oil

2 tablespoons
(1 ounce) / 30 g butter

1 medium yellow
onion, chopped

4 cloves garlic, crushed
or finely chopped

1 tablespoon
tomato paste

3 (14-ounce / 400-g)
cans chopped
tomatoes, drained

2 tablespoons
(1 ounce) / 30 g sugar

1 handful chopped
fresh basil

3 ounces / 90 g mozzarella
cheese, roughly torn

WHaT To Do:

1. Place the chicken breasts in a large ziplock bag and flatten with a rolling pin until they are very thin.

2. Mix the flour, salt, and pepper together with 2 tablespoons (1 ounce) / 30 g of the Parmesan on a large plate.

3. Dip each breast in the egg first, and then in the flour mixture until completely covered.

4. Heat olive oil and butter together in a large frying pan over medium heat.

5. Fry the chicken breasts until golden brown, about 2–3 minutes per side. Remove from pan and keep warm.

6. In the same frying pan, sauté the onions and garlic for 2 minutes until soft then add the tomato paste, chopped tomatoes, sugar, and half of the basil. Season with salt and pepper and simmer uncovered for 20 minutes.

7. Heat the broiler / grill to medium high.

8. Pour the tomato sauce into a shallow 9 x 9-inch / 25 x 25-cm ovenproof dish and carefully lay the chicken over it. Top chicken with mozzarella, remaining basil, and Parmesan, and broil / grill for 5 minutes until all the cheese has melted. Serve with salad and some pasta or potatoes.

Chicken Kebabs

Nothing says summer like these kebabs; grill them indoors or outside on the barbecue. Experiment with different vegetables, if you like.

Serves 4

You will need:

2 boneless, skinless
chicken breasts

2 red bell peppers

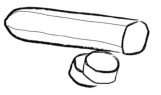

1 large zucchini

Juice and zest of 1 lime

1 tablespoon
canola oil

1 clove garlic, chopped
and crushed

1/2 teaspoon
smoked paprika

Chile
Flakes

1/2 teaspoon
dried chile flakes

Salt and pepper,
to taste

1 cup (8 ounces) /
225 g cherry tomatoes

What to Do:

1. Cut the chicken, bell peppers, and zucchini into chunks about the same size. Set aside the vegetables.

2. In a large bowl, mix together the lime juice, zest, and oil and add the garlic, paprika, chile flakes, salt, and pepper. Add the chicken and marinate in the refrigerator for at least 15 minutes and up to 1 hour.

3. On metal or wooden* skewers, thread 1 piece chicken, 1 piece bell pepper, 1 piece zucchini, a whole cherry tomato, and then another piece chicken. Follow this pattern until you have filled 2 skewers per person.

4. Heat the broiler / grill to medium high, and grill the skewers for around 5–10 minutes on each side, or until the chicken is cooked through. Serve with a fresh salad or over rice.

*If you use wooden skewers, soak in a bowl of water before using to keep them from burning.

CREAMY CHICKEN AND MUSHROOM DELIGHT

This really creamy and filling dish is ready in less than an hour. The mustard and butter are the keys to this sauce.

Serves 4

You will need:

2 tablespoons
(1 ounce) / 30 g butter

1 medium yellow
onion, chopped

1 stalk celery

2 cups (1 pound) / 450 g
diced chicken breast

1 cup (8 ounces) /
225 g sliced button
mushrooms

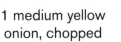

¼ cup (2 ounces) /
60 g flour

1 tablespoon
Dijon mustard

1 cup (8 ounces) /
250 ml chicken stock

½ cup (4 ounces) /
125 ml milk

Salt and pepper,
to taste

¼ cup (2 ounces) / 50 g
chopped fresh cilantro

1 cup (8 ounces) /
225 g spinach leaves

Cooked rice

WHAT TO DO:

1. Melt the butter in a large saucepan. Add the onion and celery and cook for 5 minutes until softened.

2. Add the chicken and mushrooms. Cook until the chicken starts to turn golden.

3. Stir in the flour and mustard then gradually add the chicken stock, stirring constantly. Add salt and pepper and bring to a boil. Cover with a lid and reduce heat to low.

4. Uncover, add the milk, and simmer for 15–20 minutes, or until the sauce has thickened.

5. Stir in the cilantro and the spinach and cook until the leaves have completely wilted into the sauce. Serve immediately over rice.

CHICKEN STIR-FRY

Fresh, fast, and good for you. You can substitute any of the vegetables with others you may prefer; mushrooms, broccoli, and spinach all work. Alternatively you can serve with rice instead of noodles.

Serves 4

YOU WILL NEED:

6 green onions, trimmed

1 thumb-size piece fresh gingerroot, peeled

4 carrots, peeled

2 bell peppers, any color

1 clove garlic

1 red onion

12 ounces / 350 g chicken breasts

12 ounces / 350 g dried egg noodles

3 tablespoons (1 ½ ounces) / 45 ml sesame or olive oil

1 cup (8 ounces) / 225 g snow peas

1 tablespoon fish sauce

4 tablespoons (2 ounces) / 60 ml dark soy sauce

1 teaspoon dried chile flakes

2 tablespoons (1 ounce) / 30 g unsalted cashews

Fresh cilantro leaves, to garnish

What to Do:

1. Slice the green onions into short lengths and the gingerroot into matchsticks. Cut the carrots and bell peppers into thin sticks, and slice the garlic and onion. Slice the chicken into thin strips across the grain.

2. Cook the noodles in boiling water according to package directions. Drain and toss with a little bit of oil; set aside.

3. Heat a wok or large frying pan over a high heat until very hot.

4. Add the oil and then the green onions, garlic, and gingerroot, stirring for about 1 minute, until coated in oil.

5. Add the carrots, red onion, snow peas, and bell peppers and stir-fry for 1–2 minutes.

6. Add the chicken and continue stirring until cooked through and starting to brown.

7. Pour in the fish sauce, soy sauce, and chile flakes, coating the vegetables and chicken evenly; let bubble for 2 minutes.

8. Add the noodles and cashews and toss to mix. Add more soy sauce if you like. Serve immediately, garnished with the cilantro.

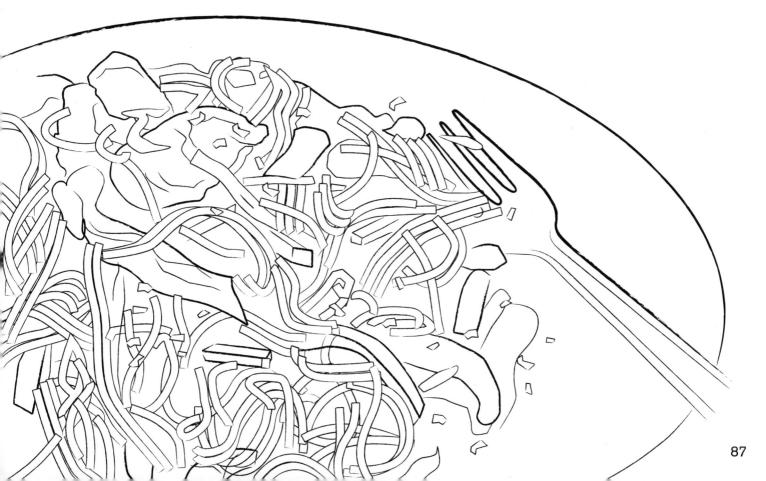

CHICKEN POT PIE

Pastry needn't be time consuming and messy—ready-to-bake puff pastry is perfect for this quick and comforting pie. You can also make extra filling and freeze it to use later as a casserole with rice.

Serves 6

You will need:

2 tablespoons
(1 ounce) / 30 g butter

1 large white
onion, diced

2 stalks celery, diced

4 ounces / 115 g
baby leeks, diced

5 ounces / 145 g
button mushrooms

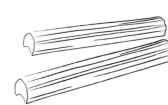

4 skinless, boneless
chicken breasts or skinless,
boneless thighs, cubed

4 tablespoons
(2 ounces) / 60 g flour

2 cups (16 ounces) /
500 ml hot chicken stock

2 tablespoons (1 ounce) /
30 g Dijon mustard

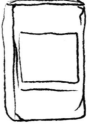

½ cup (4 ounces) /
125 ml heavy cream

½ (14-ounce / 375-g) package
ready-to-bake puff pastry

1 egg, beaten

WHAT TO DO:

1. Melt the butter in a large saucepan on low heat, adding the onion, celery, and leeks. Cook for 5 minutes until softened. Add the mushrooms and cook for a few more minutes.

2. Add the chicken to the pan, turning the heat up to medium, and cook for about 5 minutes.

3. Add the flour, and then gradually add the chicken stock, stirring well. Bring to a boil, and simmer for 5 minutes. Add the mustard and cream, simmering for another 5 minutes.

4. Remove from heat and leave to cool.

5. Preheat oven to 425 degrees F / 220 degrees C / gas mark 7.

6. Unroll the pasty and trim so it is 1 inch larger all around than your pie pan.

7. Pour your chicken mixture into the pan and set the pastry lid on top, pressing around the edges to seal. If there is any excess pastry, trim it off. Cut a 1-inch vent in the center, and brush the egg over the pastry.

8. Bake for 25–30 minutes, or until the pastry has puffed and is golden brown.

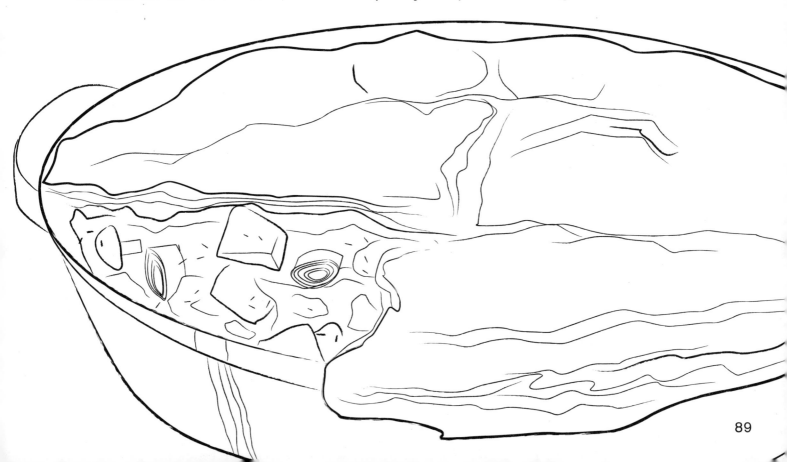

CHICKEN KORMA

An Indian classic, this fragrant and creamy dish with a hint of spice is a lot of fun to make.

Serves 4

YOU WILL NEED:

4 skinless, boneless chicken breasts

1 thumb-size piece fresh gingerroot, peeled

4 cloves garlic

Freshly ground black pepper, to taste

2 tablespoons (1 ounce) / 30 g plain yogurt

1 tablespoon canola oil

2 large yellow onions, finely chopped

12 cardamom pods, seeds crushed

1 tablespoon ground cumin

1 tablespoon ground coriander

1 teaspoon garam masala

1 teaspoon ground turmeric

1/4 teaspoon dried chile flakes

1 bay leaf

1 tablespoon all-purpose flour

2 teaspoons super-fine sugar

1/2 teaspoon fine sea salt

1 (12-ounce / 350-g) can coconut milk

1 tablespoon lemon juice

1 handful fresh cilantro

WHAT TO DO:

1. Dice the chicken and place in a non-metallic bowl. Finely grate the gingerroot and garlic, and add to the bowl with the pepper and yogurt. Stir until evenly coated, cover with plastic wrap, and marinate in the refrigerator for 2–6 hours.

2. Heat the oil in a large saucepan and slowly sauté the onions over a low heat for 15 minutes, stirring occasionally. Stir in the crushed cardamom seeds, cumin, coriander, garam masala, turmeric, chile flakes, and bay leaf. Cook the spices with the onions for 5 minutes, making sure they don't stick to the pan.

3. Stir in the flour, sugar, and salt then add the chicken with the marinade. Sauté for 10 minutes until the chicken starts to turn brown.

4. Slowly add the coconut milk to the pan, stirring together. Bring to a boil, lower the heat and cover; simmer for 15 minutes.

5. Remove from heat, remove the bay leaf, and stir in the lemon juice and most of the cilantro. Serve with the rest of the cilantro as garnish on top with rice or naan bread.

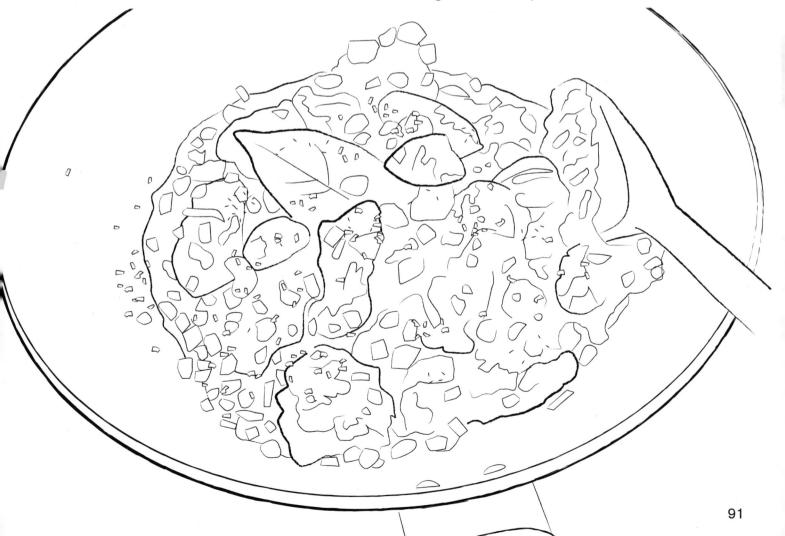

Roast Chicken

A crucial dish in a cook's arsenal, the humble roast chicken is the centerpiece of family Sunday get-togethers. This recipe is something everyone will love. Serve with your favorite vegetables.

Serves 4

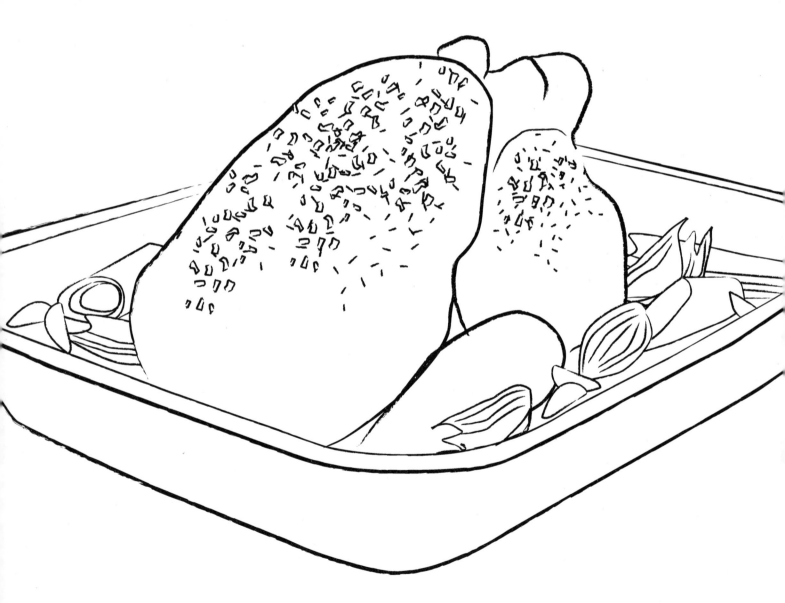

You will need:

 1 bulb garlic

 2 white onions, peeled

 2 carrots, peeled

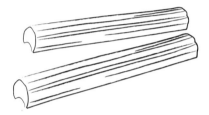 2 stalks celery

 1 (3-pound / 1.4-kg) free-range chicken

 Sea salt, to taste

 Freshly ground black pepper, to taste

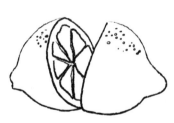 1 lemon, halved

 Small bunch each fresh thyme, rosemary, and sage

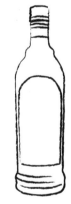 4 tablespoons (2 ounces) / 60 ml olive oil

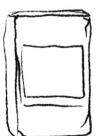 1 tablespoon all-purpose flour

 2 cups (16 ounces) / 500 ml chicken stock

WHAT TO DO:

1. Preheat oven to 375 degrees F / 190 degrees C / gas mark 5.

2. Break the garlic bulb into unpeeled cloves and roughly chop all the vegetables.

3. Layer garlic and vegetables in the bottom of a large roasting pan—big enough so the chicken will fit fairly snug.

4. Season the cavity of the chicken with salt and pepper and stuff with the lemon halves and herbs. Place the chicken on the vegetables and drizzle the chicken and vegetables with olive oil; season well with salt and pepper, rubbing it all over the bird.

5. Bake for 1 hour and 20 minutes, or until the juices run clear.

6. Remove from oven and lift the chicken to a dish or cutting board, covering with aluminum foil; let it rest for 15–20 minutes. Let any juices from the chicken pour out of the cavity into the roasting pan, as this will add to the gravy.

7. Remove the vegetables from the pan and set aside.

8. Place the roasting pan with all the juices in it over low heat; stir in the flour and simmer until it starts to thicken. Gradually pour in the stock, stirring constantly, and simmer for 5 minutes. Pour the gravy through a sieve into a small saucepan and keep on a low heat until you are ready to serve the chicken and vegetables.

Pot Roast

An easy, all-in-one pot way of cooking a flavorsome, tender roast; the vegetables and gravy are cooked together so all that's needed is a few hours while it does its thing.

Serves 4

You will need:

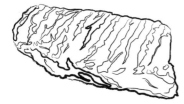
1 (3½–4-pound / 1.5-kg well-marbled beef shoulder or boneless chuck

2 tablespoons (1 ounce) / 30 ml olive or vegetable oil

Salt and pepper, to taste

Dried herbs such as thyme, basil, or sage

8 young carrots

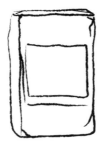
3–4 large sweet potatoes

2 large white onions

3 cups (24 ounces) / 750 ml beef stock, divided

2 tablespoons (1 ounce) / 30 g flour

2 tablespoons (1 ounce) / 30 g tomato paste

1 tablespoon brown sugar

4 cloves garlic, peeled

2 bay leaves

WHƏT TO DO:

1. Remove roast from refrigerator and bring to room temperature.

2. Heat oven to 320 degrees F / 160 degrees C / gas mark 3. Use a heavy-bottom ovenproof pot with a lid that is large enough to hold the meat and vegetables.

3. Rub the meat with the oil, salt, pepper, and dried herbs.

4. Heat the pot over medium heat and brown each side of the roast for about 5 minutes. Remove and set aside.

5. Cut the tops off the carrots and cut the sweet potatoes into 2-inch / 5-cm cubes. Roughly slice the onions and add to the pot (leaving the oil and juices) and sauté for about 5 minutes, until they begin to soften.

6. Add 2 cups (16 ounces) / 500 ml beef stock and boil for 2 minutes. Stir in the flour, tomato paste, and brown sugar and simmer for 1 minute.

7. Remove from heat, place the roast back into the pot, and place the garlic, carrots, sweet potatoes, and bay leaves around the sides. Pour the remaining beef stock over the roast and vegetables, cover, and place in the oven for 15 minutes.

8. Lower temperature to 250 degrees F / 130 degrees C / gas mark $1/2$ and cook for 1 hour.

9. Turn the heat down again to 225 degrees F / 100 degrees C / gas mark $1/4$ and cook for another $2^1/2$–3 hours.

10. Remove the roast from the pan and rest on a cutting board for about 15 minutes before carving and serving. Serve out the vegetables then spoon the gravy from the pot over the meat.

BEEF STEW

A slow-cooking, filling, and warming stew, this recipe is best for long winter nights when you need some comfort. Chuck or brisket beef is perfect for this recipe, as the long cooking time really brings out the flavors and tenderizes the meat.

Serves 6

YOU WILL NEED:

2 large white onions

3 large potatoes

½ butternut squash

2 large carrots

3 sprigs thyme, divided

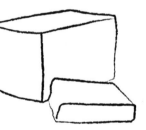

2 tablespoons (1 ounce) / 30 g butter

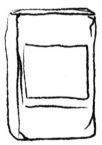

2 tablespoons (1 ounce) / 30 g flour

2 tablespoons (1 ounce) / 30 g tomato paste

3 cups (24 ounces) / 750 ml hot beef stock

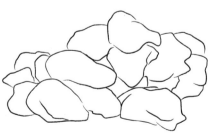

2 pounds / 1 kg stewing beef, cut into chunks

5 bay leaves

WHAT TO DO:

1. Preheat oven to 320 degrees F / 160 degrees C / gas mark 3.

2. Dice the onions and peel and chop the potatoes, squash, and carrots into large chunks.

3. Put the onions, potatoes, squash, carrots, and 1 sprig of thyme in a large ovenproof cooking pot with the butter. Heat over low to soften vegetables for 15 minutes then stir in the flour and tomato paste until everything is coated and has been absorbed.

4. Gradually stir in the beef stock then add the beef and bring to a gentle simmer, adding the bay leaves and remaining thyme.

5. Cover and place in the oven for 2$\frac{1}{2}$ hours.

6. Uncover and stir, adding boiling water if it looks a little dry. Cook for another 45 minutes, or until the meat is really tender. Serve with fresh crusty bread.

CHILI CON CARNE

This classic spicy dish is exactly what you need to warm you and your friends on a cold day. It tastes even better the day after it's made.

Serves 4

You will need:

1 tablespoon olive oil

1 large red onion, peeled and chopped

2 red bell peppers, seeded and chopped

2 cloves garlic, peeled and chopped

1 heaped teaspoon hot chili powder

1 teaspoon ground cumin

1 pound / 450 g lean ground beef

1 beef bouillon cube

1 cup (8 ounces) / 250 ml boiling water

1 teaspoon paprika

1 teaspoon sugar

Salt and pepper, to taste

2 tablespoons (1 ounce) / 30 g tomato paste

1 (14-ounce / 400-g) can chopped tomatoes

1 (14-ounce / 400-g) can kidney beans

Cooked rice

Sour cream

WHAT TO DO:

1. Heat the oil in a large pan over medium heat.

2. Sauté the onion until slightly translucent. Add the bell peppers, garlic, chili powder, paprika, and cumin. Stir well and continue sautéing for another 5 minutes, stirring occasionally.

3. Turn the heat up, add the ground beef, and brown until cooked through. Drain any excess grease, if necessary.

4. Crumble the bouillon cube into the water and let dissolve. Pour into the pan along with the chopped tomatoes.

5. Add the sugar, salt, and pepper. Stir in tomato paste until well combined. Bring to a boil, stir, and cover.

6. Turn down the heat and let simmer for 20 minutes. Check and stir occasionally, adding a dash of water if it looks dry.

7. Drain and rinse the beans, add to the pan, and bring to boil again for another 10 minutes. Season to taste.

8. Let chili stand for 10 minutes before serving to meld flavors. Serve over rice with a dollop of sour cream.

ONE-POT SAUSAGE CASSEROLE

For when you don't want a mountain of washing-up; cook this filling and warming dish in one pan, and serve with potatoes or rice.

Serves 4

YOU WILL NEED:

1 tablespoon vegetable oil

1 (1-pound / 450-g) package good-quality sausages

2 large red onions, sliced

1/2 cup (4 ounces) / 125 ml vegetable stock

1 (14-ounce / 400-g) can chopped tomatoes

1 tablespoon tomato paste

Dried chile flakes, to taste
Dried mixed herbs, to taste

1 (14-ounce / 400-g) can kidney beans

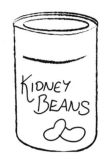

WHAT TO DO:

1. Heat the oil in a deep frying pan or wide shallow saucepan.

2. Add the sausages and onions and fry for 8–10 minutes, turning the sausages often, until the onions are caramelized.

3. Add the stock, and stir. Allow the mixture to bubble for 3–4 minutes, so it thickens a little.

4. Add the chopped tomatoes, tomato paste, chile flakes, and herbs and stir.

5. Drain and rinse the beans and stir in.

6. Turn the heat down to low, cover, and let simmer for 20–30 minutes, stirring occasionally. The sauce should thicken to form a rich gravy. Serve with potatoes or rice.

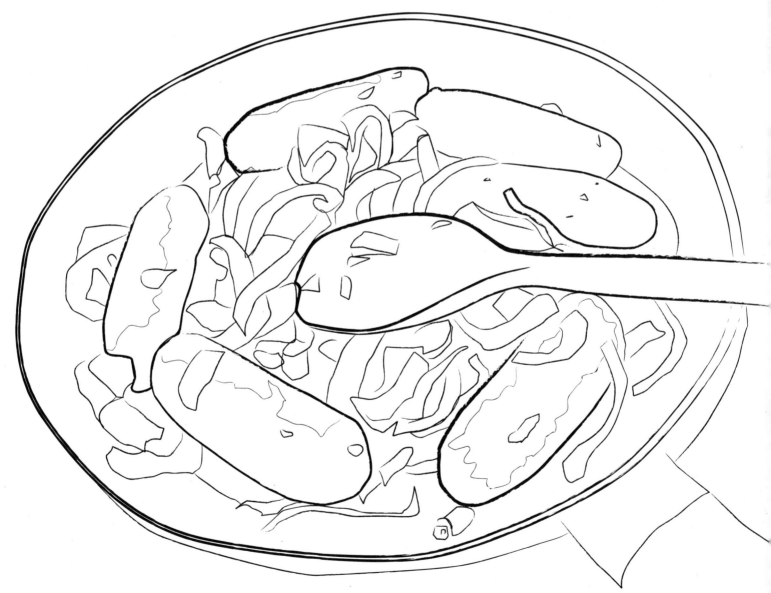

SLOPPY JOE BAKE

This is something different you can do with your standard Bolognese or chili beef. It is also a perfect way of using up slightly stale bread.

Serves 4

You will need:

1 tablespoon olive oil

2 white onions, peeled and chopped

4 cloves garlic, peeled and chopped

1 pound / 450 g ground beef

1 tablespoon ground cumin

1 handful fresh cilantro, chopped

2 teaspoons mild chili powder

1 (14-ounce / 400-g) can chopped tomatoes

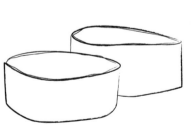

1 slightly stale baguette or loaf of crusty bread

¾ cup (3 ounces) / 90 g grated cheddar cheese

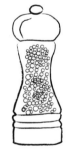

Freshly ground black pepper, to taste

What to Do:

1. Heat the oil in a large saucepan over low heat and add the onions and garlic, slowly cooking until they begin to brown.

2. Add the beef and cook until browned, draining off the grease if necessary.

3. Add the cumin, cilantro, chili powder, and tomatoes; bring to a boil and simmer for 20 minutes.

4. Preheat oven to 400 degrees F / 200 degrees C / gas mark 6.

5. After the sauce has cooked down, pour into a 9 x 12-inch / 25 x 30-cm ovenproof dish.

6. Slice the bread and arrange over the top then cover with cheese and a sprinkling of pepper.

7. Bake for 15 minutes, or until the cheese is bubbling and golden.

Perfect Pork Chops

You can just fry pork chops and eat them, but taking a little care and adding these extra ingredients turns this into a really special meat dish. The gravy is thick and comforting, and tastes great served with your favorite vegetables or mashed potatoes.

Serves 4

You will need:

4 pork loin chops, at room temperature

2 tablespoons (1 ounce) / 30 ml olive oil

8 sage leaves

Sea salt and freshly ground black pepper, to taste

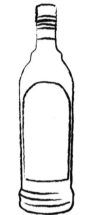

4 cloves garlic

¼ cup (2 ounces) / 60 ml apple cider or apple juice

¼ cup (2 ounces) / 60 ml vegetable stock

1 tablespoon balsamic vinegar

1 tablespoon heavy cream

1 teaspoon Dijon mustard

WHAT TO DO:

1. Make small cuts into the fat on the chops and drizzle with olive oil. Press a sage leaf into both sides of the chops then season with the salt and pepper.

2. Heat a large frying pan over medium heat and brown the chops for 7 minutes on the first side.

3. Peel each clove of garlic and flatten with the side of a knife then fry alongside the chops.

4. Turn the chops over and cook for 5 minutes or longer if they are thicker than $1\frac{1}{4}$ inches / 32 cm. Brown well on both sides.

5. Deglaze the skillet with the cider, scraping up any browned bits from the pan. Add the stock and balsamic vinegar, cover, and simmer for 10 minutes.

6. Remove the chops from the pan to rest. Discard the sage leaves and garlic. Add the cream and mustard to the gravy in the pan to thicken and serve over the chops.

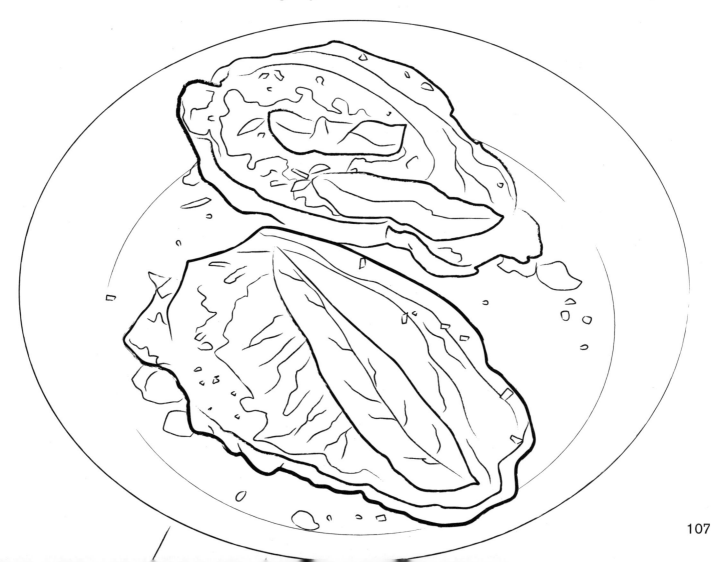

STICKY BARBECUE RIBS

Everyone's favorite barbecue essential can also be cooked in the oven if the weather is not cooperating. These are wonderfully sticky and messy, but the sauce is very easy to make; they just need a bit of time in the oven.

Serves 8

YOU WILL NEED:

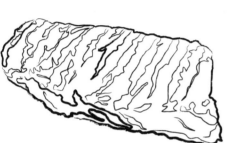

4 pounds / 1.8 kg pork belly ribs

2 (12-ounce / 350-ml) cans cola

4 tablespoons (2 ounces) / 60 ml sweet chili sauce

4 tablespoons (2 ounces) / 60 ml honey

4 tablespoons (2 ounces) / 60 ml cider vinegar

4 tablespoons (2 ounces) / 60 ml soy sauce

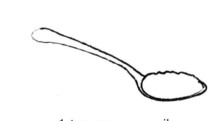

8 tablespoons (4 ounces) / 115 g ketchup

1 teaspoon paprika

4 tablespoons (2 ounces) / 60 ml canola oil

1 tablespoon chile flakes

2 teaspoons sesame seeds

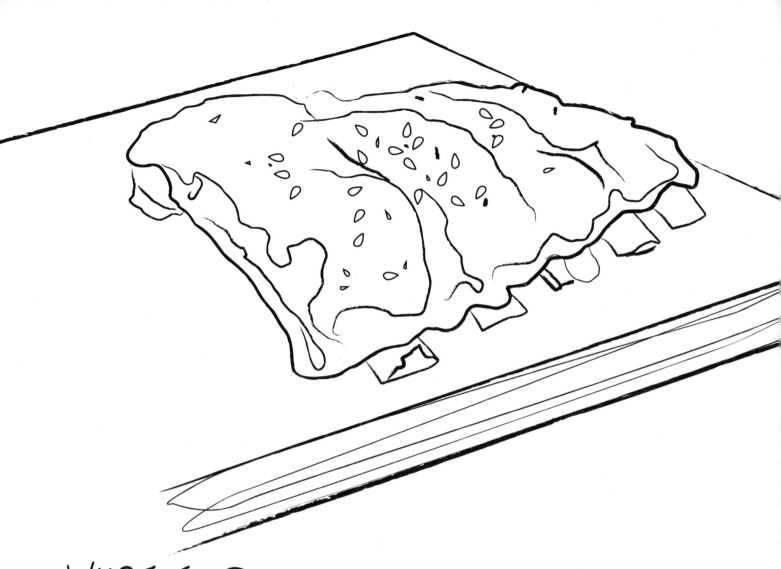

WHaT To Do:

1. Heat oven to 350 degrees F / 180 degrees C / gas mark 6.

2. Put the ribs into a roasting pan and pour the cola over the ribs, adding water, if needed, to cover the ribs entirely. Cover the pan tightly with aluminum foil and roast for 2 hours.

3. Remove from oven, drain the liquids, and lay the ribs on paper towels to dry.

4. In a small bowl, mix together the remaining ingredients, except the sesame seeds.

5. Place the ribs back in the roasting pan and pour the sauce over them, making sure they are evenly coated. Return to the pan to the oven.

6. Turn the oven up by 20 degrees and cook for 30 minutes, turning the ribs and basting every 10 minutes with any remaining sauce during cooking.

7. When ribs are sticky and crisping on the outside, remove from oven and sprinkle sesame seeds over top; slice to serve.

SWEET TREATS

BANANA BREAD

This is not only delicious, but also really quick and easy to make. It is a perfect way of using up any bananas that are past their prime.

Serves 8

YOU WILL NEED:

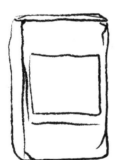

½ cup (4 ounces) / 115 g softened butter

¾ cup (6 ounces) / 175 g super-fine sugar

3 ripe bananas

½ teaspoon vanilla extract

1 cup (8 ounces) / 225 g self-rising flour

1 teaspoon baking soda

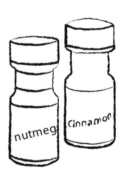

½ teaspoon ground nutmeg
½ teaspoon ground cinnamon

2 tablespoons (1 ounce) / 30 ml milk

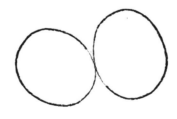

2 large eggs

WHaT TO DO:

1. Preheat oven to 350 degrees F / 180 degrees C / gas mark 4.

2. Lightly grease a 2-pound / 1-kg loaf pan and line the bottom and sides with parchment paper.

3. In a large bowl, beat the butter and sugar together until well combined. Cut the bananas into the sugar mixture and mash together with a fork. Add the vanilla.

4. Sift the flour, baking soda, nutmeg, and cinnamon into another large bowl. Combine the banana mixture into the dry mix with a wooden spoon, adding the milk and eggs, until smooth.

5. Pour the mixture into the pan and level the surface. Bake for about 50 minutes, or until golden brown. The loaf is ready if a knife inserted into the middle comes out clean. Leave to cool in the pan for about 15 minutes then turn out, peel off the parchment, and finish cooling on a wire rack.

Chocolate Orange Cupcakes

These moist and irresistible cupcakes hide a secret—using boxed cake mix means they're ready before you know it, and the frosting is also incredibly easy. They won't be around for long!

Makes 12

You will need:

1 box chocolate cake mix

Eggs and oil as per cake mix instructions

Zest and juice of 2 oranges

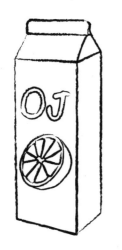

Orange juice, as needed

8 ounces / 225 g white chocolate

⅝ cup (5 ounces) / 145 g full-fat cream cheese

114

WHAT TO DO:

1. Preheat oven to 400 degrees F / 200 degrees C / gas mark 6. Prepare a 12-cup muffin tin with cupcake liners.

2. Follow the instructions on the cake mix box, using eggs and oil as listed on the directions, and replace any liquid ingredients with the orange juice—top up with additional orange juice to the correct amount needed if you don't have enough from the oranges. Add half the zest.

3. Spoon batter into cupcake liners and bake for 20 minutes. Remove and place onto wire racks. Let cupcakes cool completely before frosting.

4. In a small saucepan, melt the white chocolate over a very low heat. Place the cream cheese into a bowl and slowly add the melted chocolate to the cream cheese, stirring together until smooth. Allow to cool then refrigerate for an hour.

5. Use a flat knife, or a piping bag if you have one, to frost the cakes. Cover each cupcake top completely with frosting then sprinkle some of the remaining orange zest over the top.

Lemon Cake Squares

This is a basic sponge recipe that can be adapted very easily—try an orange variation or topping with fresh fruit. Omit the cream if you like a basic, lemony sponge cake.

Makes 16

You will need:

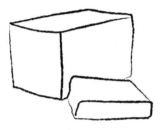

¾ cup (6 ounces) /
175 g butter, softened

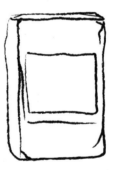

¾ cup (6 ounces) /
175 g super-fine sugar

3 eggs

Zest and juice
of 1 lemon

1 teaspoon
vanilla extract

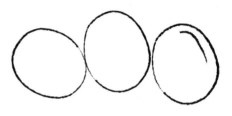

1 cup (8 ounces) / 225 g
all-purpose flour

2 teaspoons
baking powder

1 tablespoon
poppy seeds

1 cup (8 ounces) /
250 ml heavy cream

What to Do:

1. Preheat the oven to 350 degrees F / 180 degrees C / gas mark 4. Grease and line a 7 x 11-inch / 18 x 28-cm baking pan.

2. Cut the butter into pieces, and place into a large bowl with the sugar. Using the back of a wooden spoon, cream together until you get a smooth paste.

3. Add the eggs, one at a time, mixing well. Add the lemon zest, juice, and vanilla. Slowly add the flour and baking powder, stirring constantly until you have a pale and creamy batter; lastly add in the poppy seeds.

4. Pour the mix into the prepared baking pan and bake for 25–30 minutes until well risen. Once cooled, cut into 16 squares.

5. Split each square into two halves, whip the cream until thick, and fill each square; put back together then top with more cream.

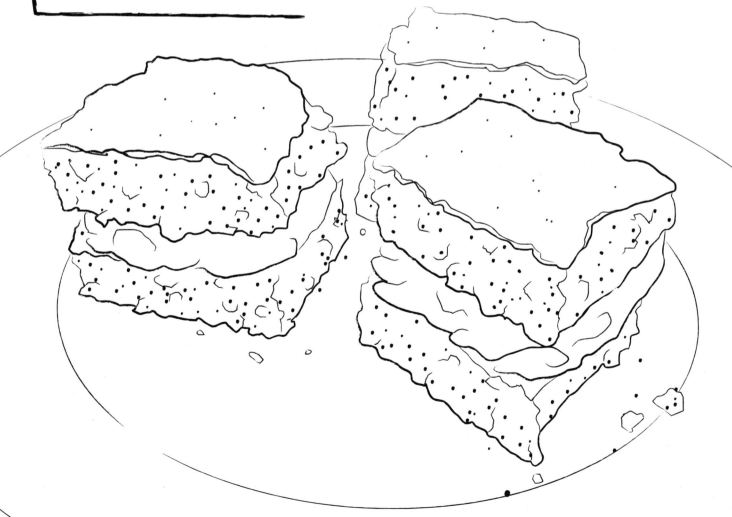

CAKE MIX WAFFLES

If you've got a waffle maker but barely use it because making batter is such a chore, this is the recipe for you. Who knew cake mix could be so versatile?

Serves 4

YOU WILL NEED:

1 box cake mix, any flavor

1 cup (8 ounces) / 250 ml water

⅓ cup (3 ounces) / 75 ml vegetable oil

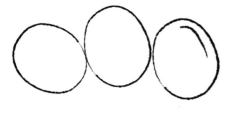

3 eggs

Choice of topping

WHAT TO DO:

1. Heat waffle maker. If it isn't nonstick, coat with cooking spray or a bit of vegetable oil.

2. Make the cake batter as directed on the box, using the water, oil, and eggs.

3. Ladle the batter onto the hot waffle maker, ensuring all the holes are evenly filled. Close the lid and bake for about 3 minutes, or until the steam stops.

4. Repeat until you've used all your batter.

5. Serve immediately with your favorite topping. Try chocolate sauce, ice cream, or a healthy option with fruit and yogurt.

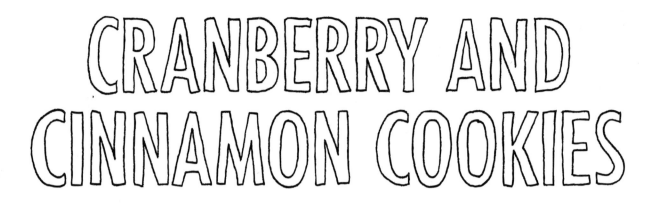

CRANBERRY AND CINNAMON COOKIES

These shortbread cookies don't seem like much, but the contrast of spicy, warming cinnamon and sweet cranberries make these a perfect winter treat.

Makes 15

You will need:

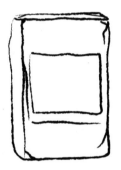

1 1/8 cups (9 ounces) /
250 g flour

1 teaspoon ground
cinnamon

Pinch of salt

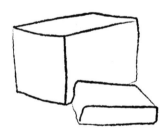

3/4 cup (6 ounces) / 175 g
butter, cut into small cubes

1/3 cup (3 ounces) /
90 g brown sugar

1 teaspoon
vanilla extract

1/2 cup (4 ounces) / 115 g
dried cranberries

2 tablespoons (1 ounce) /
30 g chopped nuts of choice

WHƏT TO DO:

1. Preheat oven to 350 degrees F / 180 degrees C / gas mark 4. Lightly grease a large baking sheet, or two if needed.

2. In a medium bowl, mix together the flour, cinnamon, and salt. Add the butter and cut it into the flour with a pastry cutter, forks, or your hands until the mix resembles breadcrumbs.

3. Add the sugar and mix until it starts to bind together. Add the vanilla, cranberries, and nuts and work together to create a dough.

4. Form the cookies by rolling the dough into a long roll about 3 inches / 8 cm in diameter. Slice cookies about $^1/_2$ inch / 2 cm thick.

5. Place onto prepared baking sheets and bake for about 20 minutes, or until they turn a light golden color. Remove from oven and let cool on baking sheet for a few minutes before transferring to a wire rack to finish cooling.

Chocolate Cookie Nuggets

These were a childhood favorite of mine and I still love making them now. No baking needed, just patience while you're waiting for them to set in the fridge.

Makes 16

YOU WILL NEED:

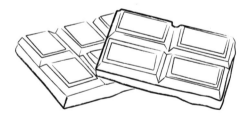

8 ounces / 225 g
chocolate chip cookies

4 tablespoons
(2 ounces) / 60 g butter

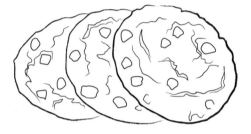

6 ounces / 170 g milk chocolate

2 tablespoons
(1 ounce) / 30 ml honey

1 teaspoon
vanilla extract

¼ cup (2 ounces) /
60 g chocolate chips

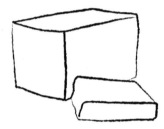

16 whole pecans

WHaT TO DO:

1. Grease and line a 7-inch / 18-cm square cake pan with parchment paper. Place the cookies in a ziplock bag or between plastic wrap and crush them into crumbs; a rolling pin works well.

2. In a medium saucepan, melt the butter and chocolate over low heat; add the honey. Stir in the cookie crumbs, vanilla, and chocolate chips and mix thoroughly until completely coated.

3. Pour the mix into the prepared cake pan and smooth the top with a spoon. Mark into 16 even squares with a sharp knife and place a pecan in the center of each.

4. Let set until the mixture is cool then place in the refrigerator for 2 hours to set completely. Once solid, cut into squares and remove from the pan. These will keep for 3 days in an airtight container.

ROCKY ROAD BARS

A chunky, chocolaty treat—substitute different dried fruits or nuts until you find a combination you love. The addition of salty peanuts on top complements the intense sweetness.

Makes 12

YOU WILL NEED:

9 ounces / 255 g
chocolate chip cookies

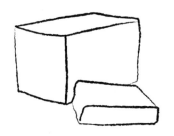

1 cup (8 ounces) / 225 g plus
2 tablespoons (1 ounce) /
30 g unsalted butter

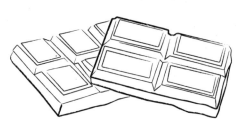

14 ounces / 410 g dark chocolate
(use the best quality you can)

½ cup (4 ounces) /
125 ml light molasses

½ cup (4 ounces) /
115 g combined dried
cherries and raisins

½ cup (4 ounces) /
115 g chopped walnuts

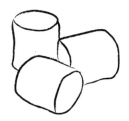

1 large handful small
marshmallows

1 ounce / 30 g whole
salted peanuts

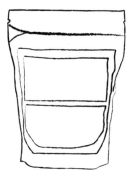

Powdered sugar,
for dusting

WHAT TO DO:

1. Grease and line a 9-inch / 25-cm square pan with parchment paper. Place the cookies in a large ziplock bag or between plastic wrap and smash into various-size pieces; a rolling pin works well. Set aside.

2. Simmer some water in a saucepan over low heat. Add the butter and chocolate to a heatproof bowl and place over hot water to gently melt. Add the molasses, stirring until well combined. Remove from heat and reserve about 1/2 cup / 225 ml.

3. Fold the cookie pieces, cherries, raisins, walnuts, and marshmallows into the chocolate mixture until all pieces are well coated.

4. Pour into the prepared pan; the surface doesn't have to be perfectly even. Pour the reserved chocolate mixture over the top to seal everything in, and sprinkle with the peanuts.

5. Refrigerate for at least 2 hours; overnight is best. Cut into 12 pieces and dust tops with powdered sugar using a sieve.

PEANUT BUTTER BROWNIES

Is there ever a better combination than chocolate and peanut butter? These moist, irresistible brownies have an extra special marbled peanut butter layer; they look impressive but are really straightforward. These definitely won't hang around for long.

Makes 16

YOU WILL NEED:

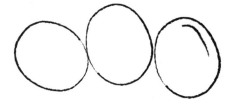

8 ounces / 225 g dark chocolate

1 ½ cups (12 ounces) / 350 g
light brown sugar, divided

1 (12-ounce / 350-g)
jar crunchy peanut
butter, divided

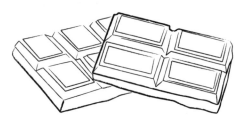

3 eggs

2 tablespoons (1 ounce)
/ 30 g cocoa powder

½ cup (4 ounces) /
115 g self-rising flour

1 teaspoon
vanilla extract

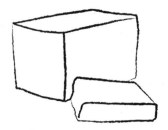

1 tablespoon butter

2 tablespoons (1 ounce) /
30 g chocolate chips

WHAT TO DO:

1. Preheat oven to 350 degrees F / 180 degrees C / gas mark 4. Grease and line a 9-inch / 25-cm square baking pan.

2. Heat a small amount of water in a saucepan so it's simmering but not boiling and place a large heatproof bowl over the top. Break the chocolate into squares and place into the bowl so it begins to melt evenly.

3. Use a wooden spoon to stir in 1 1/4 cups (10 ounces) / 285 g of brown sugar. As they begin to melt together, mix in 1 cup (8 ounces) / 225 g of the peanut butter. Stir constantly until everything has melted together.

4. Remove from the heat, keeping the water for later, and beat in the eggs, one at a time. Stir in the cocoa powder, flour, and vanilla until well combined, and then pour into the prepared pan, spreading it evenly.

5. Using the same saucepan of water and a new bowl, melt the remaining brown sugar and peanut butter together, adding in the butter. Once runny, drop spoonfuls on top of the chocolate mix then swirl with a spoon to create a marble effect.

6. Sprinkle the chocolate chips over the top and bake for 35–40 minutes. Leave to cool before cutting into squares.

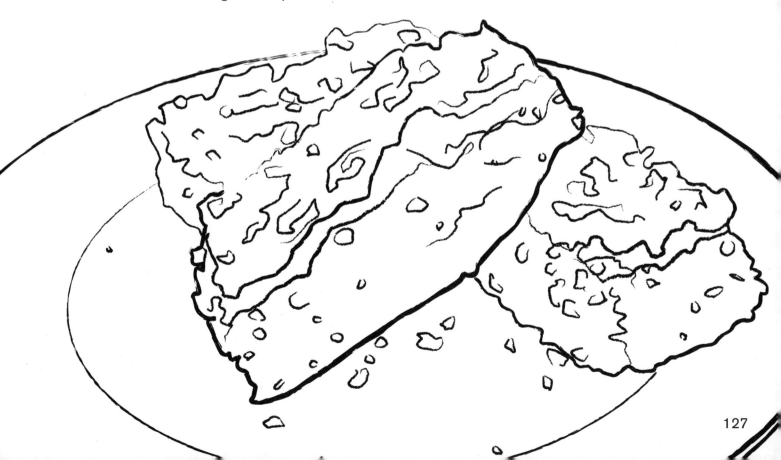

Egg-Free Chocolate Mousse

This is a really simple mousse that doesn't involve any raw eggs. You can make this the night before, but add the chocolate balls right before serving or it won't be crunchy.

Serves 4

You will need:

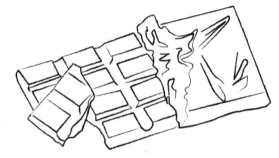

5 ounces / 145 g bittersweet chocolate

1 cup (8 ounces) / 250 ml crème fraîche (use sour cream if not available)

1 ¼ cups (10 ounces) / 310 ml heavy cream

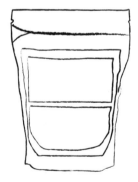

2 tablespoons (1 ounce) / 30 g powdered sugar

1–2 tablespoons (½–1 ounce) / 15–30 ml coffee (Make a cup of coffee and use the liquid.)

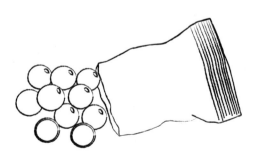

2 (1.2-ounce / 35-g) packets malted milk chocolate balls, frozen in ziplock bags

WHAT TO DO:

1. Place all the chocolate, except for one square, in a heatproof bowl over a saucepan of simmering water to melt. Add the crème fraîche to the melted chocolate and whisk until combined.

2. Place the cream and powdered sugar into a separate bowl and beat with an electric mixer until it forms soft peaks.

3. Fold the chocolate mixture into the cream, add the coffee, and stir to combine.

4. Crush the frozen chocolate balls with a rolling pin and gently fold into the mix.

5. Spoon the mousse into 4 small serving dishes and grate the remaining chocolate square over the top; serve.

STRAWBERRY CHEESECAKE

This cheesecake is a classic baked one, but it only cooks for a half hour and uses lighter ingredients than usual so it isn't too rich or sticky. Other summer berries also work perfectly with this recipe as well.

Serves 8

YOU WILL NEED:

³/₄ cup (6 ounces) / 175 g crushed graham crackers

4 tablespoons (2 ounces) / 60 g butter, melted

¹/₄ cup (2 ounces) / 60 g hazelnuts, roughly chopped

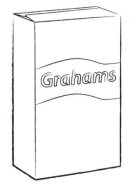

1¹/₂ cups (12 ounces) / 350 g full-fat cream cheese, softened

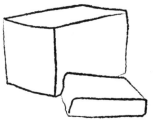

1¹/₂ cups (12 ounces) / 350 ml crème fraîche or fromage

3 eggs

³/₄ cup (6 ounces) / 175 g plus 2 tablespoons (1 ounce) / 30 g super-fine sugar

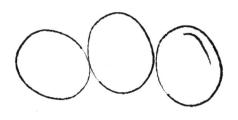

1 teaspoon vanilla extract

1¹/₂ pounds / 700 g strawberries, hulled

WHaT TO DO:

1. Preheat oven to 300 degrees F / 150 degrees C /gas mark 2. Grease and line a 9-inch / 25-cm springform pan.

2. In a small bowl, combine the crushed crackers, butter, and hazelnuts; mix well. Press the mixture into the base of the pan and place in the refrigerator to firm.

3. In a large bowl, whisk together the cream cheese, crème fraîche, eggs, ¾ cup (6 ounces) / 175 g sugar, and vanilla until very smooth.

4. Pour the mixture over the crumb base and bake for 30 minutes.

5. Place ⅓ of the strawberries into a bowl and combine with the remaining sugar; set aside.

6. Remove the cheesecake from the oven and set aside until it has completely cooled. Place onto a serving plate and refrigerate until ready to serve.

7. Purée the sugared strawberries in a blender and run through a sieve to remove the seeds. Cut the remaining strawberries into halves, arrange on top of the cheesecake, and spoon some of the purée over the top. Serve remaining purée as an optional sauce.

PEACH COBBLER

Cobblers are really easy and are a popular dessert to round off any meal. They are best served straight from the oven with some vanilla ice cream.

Serves 10

YOU WILL NEED:

4 cups (2 pounds) / 900 g fresh peach slices

1 ¼ cups (10 ounces) / 285 g sugar, divided

¼ cup (2 ounces) / 60 g brown sugar plus 1 tablespoon for sprinkling

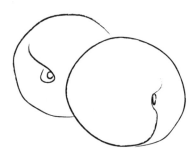

1 teaspoon cinnamon

½ teaspoon nutmeg

2 teaspoons fresh lemon juice

½ cup (4 ounces) / 125 ml water

½ cup (4 ounces) / 115 g butter

1 tablespoon baking powder

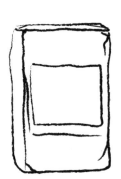

1 cup (8 ounces) / 225 g all-purpose flour

Pinch of salt

1 cup (8 ounces) / 250 ml milk

WHAT TO DO:

1. Preheat oven to 350 degrees F / 180 degrees C / gas mark 4.

2. Combine the peaches, ¼ cup (2 ounces) / 60 g sugar, ¼ cup (2 ounces) / 60 g brown sugar, cinnamon, nutmeg, lemon juice, and water in a saucepan and bring to a boil. Turn the heat down and simmer for 10 minutes, stirring every so often. Remove the syrup from the heat and let it cool.

3. Slice the butter into small pieces and place in the bottom of a 13 x 9-inch / 33 x 22-cm baking dish. Put the dish in the oven to melt the butter for 5 minutes, don't let it burn.

4. In a small bowl mix together the remaining sugar, baking powder, flour, and salt then add slowly to the milk, stirring to prevent lumps.

5. Take the baking dish from the oven and pour the batter mixture slowly over the melted butter, without stirring.

6. Spoon fruit from pan on top of the batter then gently pour syrup over everything, without stirring. The batter will rise through during cooking. Sprinkle the rest of the brown sugar over the top and place gently in the oven. Bake for 40–45 minutes. Serve fresh from the oven with vanilla ice cream.

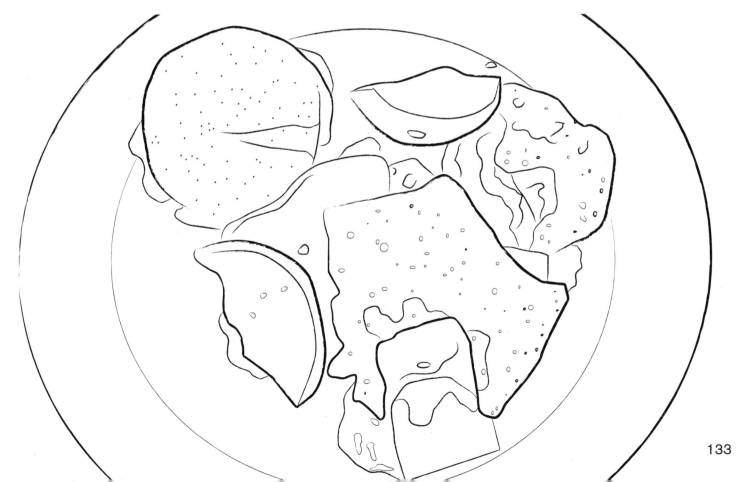

BANOFFEE PIE

Invented in England in 1972, this version of the classic recipe combines the traditional banana, caramel, and cream with a crunchy pecan base to create a real showstopper of an indulgent dessert.

Serves 8

YOU WILL NEED:

3$^1/_2$ ounces (4 ounces) / 115 g super-fine sugar

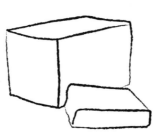

1 cup (8 ounces) / 225 g salted butter, divided

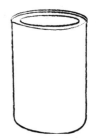

1 (14-ounce / 410-ml) can condensed milk

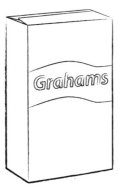

8 ounces / 225 g graham crackers

7 ounces / 200 g pecans

5–6 ripe bananas, sliced

1$^1/_3$ cups (10$^1/_2$ ounces) / 325 ml heavy cream

WHAT TO DO:

1. In a small nonstick saucepan, melt the sugar and $1/2$ cup (4 ounces) / 115 g plus 1 tablespoon butter over low heat, stirring constantly until the sugar has dissolved.

2. Add the condensed milk and bring to a rapid boil for about 3 minutes, stirring constantly for a thick golden caramel. Remove from heat and allow to cool.

3. Put the crackers in a ziplock bag or between plastic wrap and crush them into crumbs; a rolling pin works well. Roughly chop $2/3$ of the pecans, add to the cookies, and place all into a bowl.

4. Melt the rest of the butter over low heat and stir into the cookie crumbs. Press the mixture into the bottom of a 9-inch / 25-cm springform pan to create a solid base.

5. Add the bananas (reserve 8–10 slices for the top) to the cooled caramel and mix well. Pour over the base then chill in refrigerator for at least 1 hour.

6. Whip the cream until soft peaks form. Carefully remove the pie from the pan and place on a plate. Spread the cream evenly over the top of the caramel layer and top with the rest of the pecans and banana slices.

PECAN PIE

A wonderfully indulgent combination of caramel sweetness and rich nuttiness. Making your own pastry is satisfying, but a ready-made one saves time. An added step worth taking, though, is toasting the pecans beforehand; it really brings out the flavor.

Serves 8-10

You will need:

10 ounces / 285 g
pecan halves

1 (9-inch / 22-cm) prebaked pie
crust or ready-made pastry dough

½ cup (4 ounces) /
115 g dark brown sugar

¾ cup (6 ounces) /
175 ml golden syrup

¾ cup (6 ounces) /
175 ml maple syrup

6 tablespoons
(3 ounces) / 90 g butter

2 tablespoons (1 ounce) /
30 g corn flour

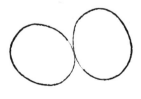

2 eggs

1 teaspoon
vanilla extract

¾ cup (6 ounces) /
175 ml half-and-half

Pinch of salt

WHαT TO DO:

1. Heat the oven to 350 degrees F / 180 degrees C / gas mark 4.

2. Spread the pecans on a lined baking sheet and bake for about 6 minutes until toasted. Allow to cool slightly then roughly crush or chop half of them.

3. If you are using a prebaked pie crust, go straight to step 5. Grease a 9-inch / 25-cm removable-bottom tart tin and roll out the pastry on a lightly floured surface to about ¼ inch / .5 cm thick. Place in the tin and chill for 30 minutes.

4. Prick the pastry base several times with a fork, line the pastry case with parchment paper, and fill with baking beans (or rice works, too). Bake for 15 minutes then remove the parchment and beans and bake for another 6 minutes until golden.

5. In a large heatproof bowl placed over a pan of simmering water, combine the sugar, golden syrup, maple syrup, and butter. Stir until melted. Remove pan from heat and set aside to cool to lukewarm, at least 15 minutes.

6. Sprinkle in the corn flour and whisk until it thickens into a smooth, silky mixture. Beat the eggs in a separate bowl then add to the cooled syrup; stir in the vanilla, half-and-half, salt, and crushed pecans.

7. Pour into the pie crust and arrange the remaining pecans on top. Bake for about 30 minutes until set; it may still wobble on top while hot. Allow to cool and set before serving.

APPLE PIE

Everyone's favorite dessert; homemade apple pie can put a smile on anyone's face. Serve while still warm with softly whipped cream.

Serves 8-10

You will need:

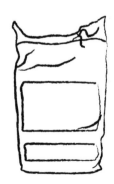

1½ cups (12 ounces) / 350 g butter, divided

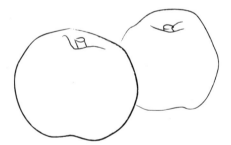

¾ cup (6 ounces) / 175 g super-fine sugar, divided plus 1 tablespoon extra for the top

2 eggs

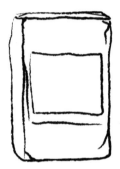

1¾ cups (14 ounces) / 400 g all-purpose flour, divided

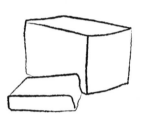

6 Bramley or Granny Smith apples

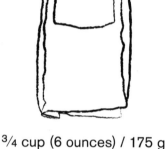

1 tablespoon ground cinnamon

½ cup (4 ounces) / 115 g light brown sugar

Pinch of salt

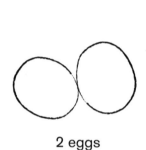

¼ cup (2 ounces) / 60 ml water

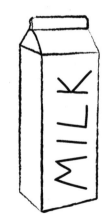

1 tablespoon milk

138

WHat to Do:

1. For the pastry, beat 1 cup (8 ounces) / 225 g of the butter and ¼ cup (2 ounces) / 50 g of the super-fine sugar in a large bowl then break in the eggs. Beat together for about 1 minute. Work in 1½ cups (12 ounces) / 350 g of the flour, a bit at a time, until it starts to firm up then finish gathering it with your hands.

2. Gently work the dough into a ball, cut in half, and form each half into a disc. Wrap in plastic wrap and chill for 45 minutes.

3. Preheat oven to 375 degrees F / 190 degrees C / gas mark 5.

4. Peel, core, quarter, and slice the apples to about ½ inch / 1 cm thick and set aside.

5. Roll out pastry so both discs are about ¼ inch / .5 cm thick, and place the bottom crust in a 9-inch / 25-cm pie pan. Fill with the apples and sprinkle the cinnamon over top.

6. Melt the remaining butter in a medium saucepan. Stir in the remaining flour to form a paste. Add the remaining super-fine sugar, the brown sugar, salt, and water; bring to a boil. Reduce the heat and simmer for 5 minutes, stirring constantly. When it has thickened, slowly and evenly pour it over the apples.

7. Place the top crust over apples, sealing the edges together with a small amount of water. If there is excess roll it under the lip. Cut steam slits in the top, paint the crust with the milk, and generously sprinkle over the extra sugar. Bake for 40–45 minutes, or until golden, then remove and let it sit for 5–10 minutes.

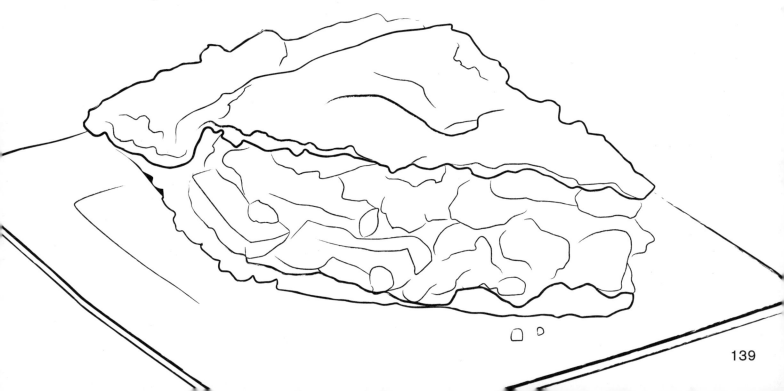

INDEX

ABOUT THE AUTHOR

Rachel Lewis is an illustrator and graphic designer currently living in London. Since graduating from the University of Wolverhampton in June 2009, she has created work for clients as diverse as the Royal Thames Yacht Club and *Cleo Magazine* in Australia, as well as working as a full-time graphic designer.

With a passion for cooking not always satisfied when living a busy city life, Rachel is always experimenting with whatever can be found in her cupboard to create quick, tasty, and cheap meals. Rachel had two illustrations published in the 2011 book, *They Draw and Cook*, prompting her to focus on drawing food (and enjoying eating it).